Heart Thoughts

As a Woman thinks in her heart so is She

STEPHANIE M. KIRKLAND

You've probably read a million self-help books but how do you apply those ideas into your life and make real and lasting changes?

The Heart Thoughts Daily Mindset Inspiration *Guide is a* guide for women on the journey of personal growth and self discovery. It has a designed to be used daily to form a mindset that inspires action & growth.

Everyday the thought provoking inspiration keeps you committed, accountable & motivated to renew your mind and intentionally reflect on how you can position your thinking for your GREATER. You can celebrate making the decision to work on you every day!

Your thought life is the beginning of self care. These inspirations can transform, shape and dynamically alter your life!

The *Heart Thoughts Daily Mindset Inspiration Guide* includes 365 days worth of powerful, actionable wisdom, truths and focus to help you discover and pursue your personal growth. It's insightful, practical, and creative—a great tool for transformation and growth! You will be well on the way to DISCOVER, BECOME and EMPOWER your life. You will gain clarity on who you are and what is holding you back. You will also streamline and bring harmony to your life so that you have the space and energy to pursue your purpose.

Everyday you will take small and manageable steps. Each step reveals aspects of yourself and tools to empower your growth. Everyday becomes a opportunity to reflect, plan and create specific actions that keep you moving forward week after week.

Through the Guide, we cover three main areas:

- Understanding more about yourself;

- Addressing thoughts that create roadblocks and limitations that
hold you back;

-- Taking actions that empower your personal growth journey.

As you do the daily Soul Clarity, you may feel uncomfortable or even sad. Don't shut down, be honest with yourself and about life. The inspiration provides information that can reveal who you are and who you need to BECOME to move forward. We need to deal with these internal limitations before we can DISCOVER, BECOME and EMPOWER our lives which creates effective IMPACT on the different roles and responsibilities we walk out on a daily basis as women.

Take your time and stay on track. You may be tempted to read ahead, trying to cram 365 days of learning and actions into less time. Believe me, I understand that. But I encourage you to "marinate" and allow the information presented to resonate in your mind, heart, soul and spirit for greater clarity and application

Be intentional. Give yourself the gift of this time and fully complete the process.

It will be great to write your reflection, so please take the time to write your thoughts and progress. It is the only way to get the most from this process.

PERSONAL COMMITTMENT

I, _____, am committed to creating meaningful and lasting change in my life and doing all of the work it requires. As part of this process I will:

1. I will write down in clear language who I want to be. I will provide details and add thoughts to these items daily.

2. I will commit to surround myself with the "right" people and limit exposure to people, things and ideas that are a risk to my success.

3. I will give myself a lot of grace

4. I will make sure I read my goals, journal and talk with supportive people every day to ensure I am making decisions and thinking thoughts that will keep me moving towards my goal.

5. I will keep moving forward EVERY SINGLE DAY.

_____
Signature

_____
Accountability Witness

MY WHY STATEMENT

Your why statement puts in perspective why you are pursuing these next 365 Days Remember, your why has to be greater than your excuses in order to succeed.

JANUARY 1

A new season doesn't "automatically" mean there is a NEW YOU. You must be willing to do the work to match your words. You CAN make it happen. It is a GREAT time for a FRESH START, but only YOU can determine that. Let this be that for you. Let's DO the work.

REFLECTION

What stands out to me in this Reflection? What do I need to Change to Live this Fully? How will I Live this Today?

JANUARY 2

Conflict EXPOSES our deepest beliefs. It passes by the surface we intentionally show everybody and "draws" out of the depths of our hearts what is there. When you are "exposed," use it as a opportunity to see your "true" self. It is no longer HIDDEN by the "good times". Work on what you see.

REFLECTION

What stands out to me in this Reflection? What do I need to Change to Live this Fully? How will I Live this Today?

JANUARY 3

There are some opportunities, relationships and situations you will NEED, but you will have to give up something (sacrifice) to GET IT! Do not allow the desire for "convenience, comfort or something being easy" to be how you determine your actions. It will HINDER you.

REFLECTION

What stands out to me in this Reflection? What do I need to Change to Live this Fully? How will I Live this Today?

JANUARY 4

Destiny and Purpose are "woven" into the very fabric of your being. God created you with the SEEDS of your gifts, talents and abilities, and NOW it is up to YOU to cultivate them so they can mature. The more you GROW and BECOME the greatest expression of yourself, the more is released into your life.

REFLECTION

What stands out to me in this Reflection? What do I need to Change to Live this Fully? How will I Live this Today?

JANUARY 5

We are sooo quick to "pass the buck or responsibility" on God or others to make us happy or fulfilled. We must really ask OURSELVES, what part do I play? What am I suppose to be doing? What do I need to change? Where have I missed it? What do I need to ask forgiveness for? Yes, God has a part BUT, so do you. What is YOUR part?

REFLECTION

What stands out to me in this Reflection? What do I need to Change to Live this Fully? How will I Live this Today?

JANUARY 6

Purpose COMPELS you to want more. When you understand your purpose, no one has to convince you to grow. It becomes necessary.

REFLECTION

What stands out to me in this Reflection? What do I need to Change to Live this Fully? How will I Live this Today?

JANUARY 7

As a woman your identity is multifaceted. You have identity as a woman, wife, sister, leader, friend, mentor, or business woman. If you understand that you have identity in these areas, your DESIRE to grow in these areas should increase. You should desire to be the greatest expression of you, because it will bring the greatest impact. You have VALUE that you bring to those connected to you in these areas. HUNGER for growth. Be willing to TAKE ACTION. If you don't understand, FIND those CALLED to teach you.

REFLECTION

What stands out to me in this Reflection? What do I need to Change to Live this Fully? How will I Live this Today?

JANUARY 8

Start looking at "why" it didn't work out. Do NOT just settle with the fact that it didn't work out. A LOT of times we MISS the lesson and REPEAT the same scenario with another person or situation when we don't. What part did you play? Even if you weren't the "main" problem, you need to ask yourself why you were "vulnerable" to that TYPE of situation.

REFLECTION

What stands out to me in this Reflection? What do I need to Change to Live this Fully? How will I Live this Today?

JANUARY 9

You can be looking sooo hard for the BIG deal/event/step that you MISS or overlook the "real and necessary" small step, which takes you where you want to go. Pay attention.

REFLECTION

What stands out to me in this Reflection? What do I need to Change to Live this Fully? How will I Live this Today?

JANUARY 10

When you always QUIT, you never get to know or experience what "could" be. You never learn how "powerful" you are. You never gain the "lessons" necessary for your next season. Don't Quit.

REFLECTION

What stands out to me in this Reflection? What do I need to Change to Live this Fully? How will I Live this Today?

JANUARY 11

Be careful changing your mind because it is going to be hard! Press through and complete the task. HARD doesn't mean impossible. Don't take the "easy way" out! You have (in you) what you need to do it!

REFLECTION

What stands out to me in this Reflection? What do I need to Change to Live this Fully? How will I Live this Today?

JANUARY 12

Your life will change when YOU make a decision to change. NO ONE is responsible to do it but you. You are waiting and waiting. Year after year is going by and you are still waiting. You are "blaming" God's "timing" as the reason. IT IS NOT GOD'S TIMING that is the issue. PLEASE accept that it is you.

REFLECTION

What stands out to me in this Reflection? What do I need to Change to Live this Fully? How will I Live this Today?

JANUARY 13

You STARE at all the wonderful programs and products on social media. YOU KNOW in your HEART it is what you need to do, but you STILL do ..... nothing. When will you be tired of being behind, broken, and unfulfilled? WHEN will you reach a point when you VALUE yourself ENOUGH to do what you need to do for you? When will you stop accepting wearing a mask when you can LIVE FREE? You say, "When my children are grown, but they need you WHOLE now. When my husband changes jobs, but he needs you WHOLE now. When I get more money, but money will come when you are WHOLE. The choice is yours.

REFLECTION

What stands out to me in this Reflection? What do I need to Change to Live this Fully? How will I Live this Today?

JANUARY 14

When excuses become your norm your goals are hindered. Eventually you look up and the date you should have been FINISHED is passed and you find yourself still at the starting line. Say to yourself, no more excuses.

REFLECTION

What stands out to me in this Reflection? What do I need to Change to Live this Fully? How will I Live this Today?

JANUARY 15

Are you "desiring" to change your life BUT notice you won't do anything about it? You're finding yourself "passively" waiting to be rescued. Unconsciously you believe that it is someone else's responsibility to do it. The real truth is no one can rescue you. You MUST rescue and take the INITIATIVE to change yourself. It's your life.

REFLECTION

What stands out to me in this Reflection? What do I need to Change to Live this Fully? How will I Live this Today?

JANUARY 16

EVERY level/season/goal in your life has a PROCESS. It doesn't "just" happen. You must EMBRACE the process if you want to get and KEEP the results.

REFLECTION

What stands out to me in this Reflection? What do I need to Change to Live this Fully? How will I Live this Today?

JANUARY 17

INSECURITY plays with your mind. It "elevates" your BAGGAGE to a level of truth and REDUCES the "real" truth to fantasy. You begin asking questions about people that ARE GOOD FOR YOU. If you don't stop the conversation, you will separate yourself from the people you NEED in your life.

REFLECTION

What stands out to me in this Reflection? What do I need to Change to Live this Fully? How will I Live this Today?

JANUARY 18

Low self esteem makes you uncomfortable around people who are doing things you want to do but are unwilling to sacrifice to get it done. You will eventually think they are "against" you, but the truth is you are convicted because of your lack of action. Stop the MIND conversation. You need these people in your life.

REFLECTION

What stands out to me in this Reflection? What do I need to Change to Live this Fully? How will I Live this Today?

JANUARY 19

BEWARE of RELATIONSHIP LEECHES!! Are you are not GROWING in your relationships (friendship, church, romantic love)? Does it FEED your "insecurity, lack, negative mindset, prey issues" ? Are they ALLOWING it to continue because it FEEDS the "insecurity, ego, predatory issues in them"? You need to come to YOURSELF and YOU NEED TO RUN!!!! They will SUCK the life out of you.
You will be dead soon (spirit/soul). Move.

REFLECTION

What stands out to me in this Reflection? What do I need to Change to Live this Fully? How will I Live this Today?

JANUARY 20

Sometimes we are drawn to people because they "express" with their life what is MISSING in ours. We find ourselves living THROUGH them instead of LEARNING from them. The problem is you never grow. You become a FOLLOWER and the LEADER in you never manifests. Are you using them to make up the difference in what you lack in yourself? Many do this with friendships, church and romantic love and it is a unhealthy connection that doesn't end well. LEARN from them. DON'T live THROUGH them.

REFLECTION

What stands out to me in this Reflection? What do I need to Change to Live this Fully? How will I Live this Today?

JANUARY 21

Creating "distance" from people that are not bringing increase in your life is not being rude. This is "life and death" to you spirit, soul and body. Who you allow in your "intimate" space IMPACTS your DESTINY! You must learn to PROTECT yourself. REPOSITION their "access" in your life and decisions.

REFLECTION

What stands out to me in this Reflection? What do I need to Change to Live this Fully? How will I Live this Today?

JANUARY 22

We CAN miss opportunities to INCREASE and LIVE a better more fulfilling life when we DENY our part in making it better. You DO have a responsibility and part to play in your SUCCESS. You must know your part.

REFLECTION

What stands out to me in this Reflection? What do I need to Change to Live this Fully? How will I Live this Today?

JANUARY 23

Stop trying to prove yourself to PEOPLE who really don't care. Stop sharing things they will just trample on with their words and actions. Why are you trying to "impress" them? Be COMFORTABLE knowing (whether they acknowledge it or not) that you are valuable.

REFLECTION

What stands out to me in this Reflection? What do I need to Change to Live this Fully? How will I Live this Today?

JANUARY 24

Refuse to ALLOW your emotions to dictate your actions. Your emotions should not be making your decisions. They are suppose to support your decisions.

REFLECTION

What stands out to me in this Reflection? What do I need to Change to Live this Fully? How will I Live this Today?

JANUARY 25

Sometimes you don't "hear" the answers because inside you know it is something
you don't want to do. You are "blocking" what could FREE you. When you "open"
yourself to "whatever you need to hear"
it usually comes.

REFLECTION

What stands out to me in this Reflection? What do I need to Change to Live this Fully? How will I Live this Today?

JANUARY 26

If God made you a 10, why are you trying to "reduce" yourself to a 5 to SATISFY the INSECURITY of someone else? Stop living according to "other people's" insecurities. Find people who want to see you SHINE!

REFLECTION

What stands out to me in this Reflection? What do I need to Change to Live this Fully? How will I Live this Today?

JANUARY 27

When you GROW, CHANGE comes. You CAN'T have one without the other. They are two sides of the same coin. As the saying goes "if you want something different you have to do something different." The question becomes, "What are you going to do?"

REFLECTION

What stands out to me in this Reflection? What do I need to Change to Live this Fully? How will I Live this Today?

JANUARY 28

You are an ORIGINAL with "seeds" of potential and possibility on the inside of you.
Don't settle for "becoming" someone else. Do the work necessary to nurture what is
ALREADY inside of you.

REFLECTION

What stands out to me in this Reflection? What do I need to Change to Live this Fully? How will I Live this Today?

JANUARY 29

Remember your perspective isn't the ONLY right perspective in a situation.
Be open to hear the another view.

REFLECTION

What stands out to me in this Reflection? What do I need to Change to Live this Fully? How will I Live this Today?

JANUARY 30

You must BE ready not GETTING ready. A lot of times you want FAVOR to intervene in your life but you are not POSITIONED to experience its effects. Don't miss out on opportunities! If you KNOW it yours, PREPARE to receive it whether you "see" it or not!

REFLECTION

What stands out to me in this Reflection? What do I need to Change to Live this Fully? How will I Live this Today?

JANUARY 31

DISTRACTIONS don't just come from the outside. You can also get distracted by your insecurities. They draw relationships and activities that REDUCE you instead of BUILD you. Do you know your "insecurities"? It is important to KNOW what can pull you AWAY from the goal/purpose.

REFLECTION

What stands out to me in this Reflection? What do I need to Change to Live this Fully? How will I Live this Today?

FEBRUARY 1

Does your relationships and activities SUPPORT your purpose? If NOT you can become distracted and the time that was FOR your purpose is lost. REFOCUS and evaluate what is going on in your space.

REFLECTION

What stands out to me in this Reflection? What do I need to Change to Live this Fully? How will I Live this Today?

FEBRUARY 2

In order to "see" what is GREAT about yourself, you have to "believe" that it is there!
If you don't believe it, you won't see it, no matter who tells you. It BEGINS within.

REFLECTION

What stands out to me in this Reflection? What do I need to Change to Live this Fully? How will I Live this Today?

FEBRUARY 3

Sometimes the LESSON and WISDOM needed to change your circumstance/
season will "require" you to ASK for help. Until you do, you will find yourself
"stuck" because you DON'T have the answer.
The answer is IN someone else. ASK.

REFLECTION

What stands out to me in this Reflection? What do I need to Change to Live this Fully? How will I Live this Today?

FEBRUARY 4

When you don't walk into your destiny you impact those attached to you. They will lack what they are suppose to be getting from you. Ask yourself what is holding you back?

REFLECTION

What stands out to me in this Reflection? What do I need to Change to Live this Fully? How will I Live this Today?

FEBRUARY 5

Don't let other people GUILT bully you about what you feel is right. Make sure you do the research and have your information clear. Choose to press forward. You are more likely to feel guilty when you are not prepared.

REFLECTION

What stands out to me in this Reflection? What do I need to Change to Live this Fully? How will I Live this Today?

FEBRUARY 6

In relationships its not always about being right or winning, its about being OPEN to listen to someone else's opinion even if you don't agree.

REFLECTION

What stands out to me in this Reflection? What do I need to Change to Live this Fully? How will I Live this Today?

FEBRUARY 7

You must get CLEAR about what you WANT so you will know what you need to RELEASE. This makes room for what you need to ADD to your life for where you are going.

REFLECTION

What stands out to me in this Reflection? What do I need to Change to Live this Fully? How will I Live this Today?

FEBRUARY 8

Just because you like someone, it doesn't automatically make them your friend.
Some people are just acquaintances. You need to know the difference.

REFLECTION

What stands out to me in this Reflection? What do I need to Change to Live this Fully? How will I Live this Today?

FEBRUARY 9

Don't get COMFORTABLE with the negative circumstances in your life (The "Oh Well" attitude) to the point that it BECOMES your "NORMAL".
It can cause you to lose your ABILITY to HOPE (expect and seek after better).

REFLECTION

What stands out to me in this Reflection? What do I need to Change to Live this Fully? How will I Live this Today?

FEBRUARY 10

Don't just QUIT because it didn't work out the way you wanted! If it is what you are suppose to be doing, DUST yourself off, put your attitude in CHECK, get your emotions LINED UP with your decision and BEGIN AGAIN.

REFLECTION

What stands out to me in this Reflection? What do I need to Change to Live this Fully? How will I Live this Today?

FEBRUARY 11

Let your circumstance be an opportunity to grow and for God to be glorified. You determine the definition of your circumstance. Let it be overcomer, steadfast, focused, and determined.

REFLECTION

What stands out to me in this Reflection? What do I need to Change to Live this Fully? How will I Live this Today?

FEBRUARY 12

It's EASY to "desire/want" something different. The REAL QUESTION is, "Are you willing to do something about it?" There is a HUGE difference.

REFLECTION

What stands out to me in this Reflection? What do I need to Change to Live this Fully? How will I Live this Today?

FEBRUARY 13

Be mindful using ASSUMPTIONS to make decisions. The truth is, you are GUESSING and don't know the truth. You miss out on sooooo much when you allow ASSUMPTION to be your "source" of information for your decisions.

REFLECTION

What stands out to me in this Reflection? What do I need to Change to Live this Fully? How will I Live this Today?

FEBRUARY 14

Whether you realize it or not, you have "trained" yourself to REACT certain ways based on your situations (when someone cuts in front of you, when someone is disrespectful, when someone speaks etc...). You must INTENTIONALLY INSPECT your reactions today. Do they HELP or HINDER you?

REFLECTION

What stands out to me in this Reflection? What do I need to Change to Live this Fully? How will I Live this Today?

FEBRUARY 15

Don't let "procrastination" keep you from your goals. A lot of times we HESITATE because it "seems" difficult. We allow ASSUMPTIONS to make our decisions instead of finding out the truth. HARD doesn't mean impossible. It just means you will need to put in some EFFORT. Put in the effort.

REFLECTION

What stands out to me in this Reflection? What do I need to Change to Live this Fully? How will I Live this Today?

FEBRUARY 16

If you give your word and commit to something and you no longer can do or go, DO NOT LET SILENCE be your RESPONSE. DO NOT SAY to yourself, "Well me not showing up should let them know I am not coming". TACKY TACKY. ALL you have is your WORD to express your "character".
Do what you say, or SAY what you CAN'T do.

REFLECTION

What stands out to me in this Reflection? What do I need to Change to Live this Fully? How will I Live this Today?

FEBRUARY 17

It is sad to live in a day and time when one's word means little and the one who gives his/her word is not "moved" or "embarrassed" that what he/she says has no value. 1. If you have given your word, don't WAIT to be reminded of your commitment. It's not their responsibility. 2. Don't leave people in the DARK about an expectation that you have committed to them. 3. Let's work at making our word our bond. 4. If you can't HOLD to it, you need to say something to them. Don't let your SILENCE be your response.

REFLECTION

What stands out to me in this Reflection? What do I need to Change to Live this Fully? How will I Live this Today?

FEBRUARY 18

Run YOUR race. Everyone goes at a different pace. Don't look at where someone else is on the track, they could have been running longer than you! Don't compare yourself to others.
FOCUS on where you are and where YOU need to go.

REFLECTION

What stands out to me in this Reflection? What do I need to Change to Live this Fully? How will I Live this Today?

FEBRUARY 19

You must learn to "release" what you have as a "seed" for what you want. BETTER is waiting. You must plant the "seed of NOW" to have the HARVEST of what is to come.

REFLECTION

What stands out to me in this Reflection? What do I need to Change to Live this Fully? How will I Live this Today?

FEBRUARY 20

What you have TODAY is the harvest of your choices from YESTERDAY. Your FUTURE is "positioned" by your CHOICES and ACTIONS TODAY. What are you waiting on? NOW is when the FUTURE is set.

REFLECTION

What stands out to me in this Reflection? What do I need to Change to Live this Fully? How will I Live this Today?

FEBRUARY 21

There is a LEVEL OF LIVING that rest in peace. Irregardless of what is going on around you, you can rest and not be moved. Why? Because you know who you are and you KNOW your truth works.

REFLECTION

What stands out to me in this Reflection? What do I need to Change to Live this Fully? How will I Live this Today?

FEBRUARY 22

Your life will change when you do. It can't do it without YOU. Sometimes we believe that everything AROUND us must change and THEN it will be better, but that is not necessary. YOU are the key.

REFLECTION

What stands out to me in this Reflection? What do I need to Change to Live this Fully? How will I Live this Today?

FEBRUARY 23

I know you have been taught not to make yourself a priority. Until you do you won't be able to LIVE in the fullness of your PURPOSE. KNOWING yourself is apart of the journey.

REFLECTION

What stands out to me in this Reflection? What do I need to Change to Live this Fully? How will I Live this Today?

FEBRUARY 24

It BEGINS within! The changes you desire and pursue will be temporary without "renewing" your mind and heart to who you need to
BECOME to maintain the change.

REFLECTION

What stands out to me in this Reflection? What do I need to Change to Live this Fully? How will I Live this Today?

FEBRUARY 25

You SAY with your mouth that you are tired, but it hasn't gotten to where it counts, your HEART. When you get tired "FOR REAL" of going through the same stuff, you WILL do something different.
You just haven't reached "SHO' NUFF" tired yet.

REFLECTION

What stands out to me in this Reflection? What do I need to Change to Live this Fully? How will I Live this Today?

FEBRUARY 26

You can't fulfill your PURPOSE and DESTINY until you know WHO you are (Identity). Knowing that you are a Spiritual ONLY deals with your IDENTITY HERITAGE. That is just one piece of the beginning. It is a FOUNDATIONAL piece but there is more. It is not a FULL EXPRESSION or picture of who you are. That's just like me saying, "I'm Black." That doesn't give you a full understanding of who I am.

REFLECTION

What stands out to me in this Reflection? What do I need to Change to Live this Fully? How will I Live this Today?

FEBRUARY 27

Remember, the LESSONS that we need are found WITHIN the JOURNEY. You master them as you go and not at the end. REFOCUS, keep your eyes open, look for the LESSON and learn it. It's important for what is coming.

REFLECTION

What stands out to me in this Reflection? What do I need to Change to Live this Fully? How will I Live this Today?

FEBRUARY 28

Doing something NEW is not always comfortable. STOP "waiting" for COMFORT to be the "SIGNAL" that it is the right decision. You're gonna miss it! There is a difference between "comfort and peace".
You can be uncomfortable BUT STILL have peace.

REFLECTION

What stands out to me in this Reflection? What do I need to Change to Live this Fully? How will I Live this Today?

MARCH 1

Process your DECISIONS. They don't just impact the "moment" and you are not the only person affected. Remember you can't "assume" what someone's reaction will be to your decision, so make sure you are confident in your choice irregardless of the outcome.

REFLECTION

What stands out to me in this Reflection? What do I need to Change to Live this Fully? How will I Live this Today?

MARCH 2

In order to stand firm in your situation you must have CONFIDENCE in your decision. Focusing on others "reactions" to your decisions slows down your progress. DOUBT steals confidence.

REFLECTION

What stands out to me in this Reflection? What do I need to Change to Live this Fully? How will I Live this Today?

MARCH 3

WHY CAN'T you have it!!! WHY CAN'T you do it!! STOP listening to people who have: 1. LIMITED themselves 2. don't want more 3. or failed and REFUSED to get up! Find someone who GOT UP to listen too and keep it moving.

REFLECTION

What stands out to me in this Reflection? What do I need to Change to Live this Fully? How will I Live this Today?

MARCH 4

Stop telling yourself that you have to put your DESIRES, PURPOSE, DREAMS, VISION and HOPES on HOLD. There is a way to have HARMONY in your life. You won't see the "way" until you believe that there IS a "way".

REFLECTION

What stands out to me in this Reflection? What do I need to Change to Live this Fully? How will I Live this Today?

MARCH 5

In order to move forward towards fulfilling your Dreams and Goals you MUST BELIEVE that your DESIRES, PURPOSE, DREAMS, VISION and HOPES are EQUAL in value to those in your realm of influence (husband, children, work, church, opportunities, friends). You are JUST AS IMPORTANT.

REFLECTION

What stands out to me in this Reflection? What do I need to Change to Live this Fully? How will I Live this Today?

MARCH 6

SUCCESS is not just about having the best "business acumen" or product. If you are not whole it will "filter" into your business and your decisions. It will "hinder" your progress. The "product" is just the beginning. SUCCESS comes through the person BEHIND the product.

REFLECTION

What stands out to me in this Reflection? What do I need to Change to Live this Fully? How will I Live this Today?

MARCH 7

No matter how great your vision/purpose, If YOU (the vessel that the vision comes thru) are not ready for it you will find yourself going in circles EVEN THO you see and know what it is.

REFLECTION

What stands out to me in this Reflection? What do I need to Change to Live this Fully? How will I Live this Today?

MARCH 8

Stop letting your excuses win.

REFLECTION

What stands out to me in this Reflection? What do I need to Change to Live this Fully? How will I Live this Today?

MARCH 9

When you know your VALUE and what you "bring to the table", you will STOP
obligating yourself to things just because you can do them.
Those you connect with will benefit because you are
functioning out of your PURPOSE.

REFLECTION

What stands out to me in this Reflection? What do I need to Change to Live this Fully? How will I Live this Today?

MARCH 10

Being BUSY is not a correct "reader" for being EFFECTIVE. We sometimes think it means multi tasking. BUSY doesn't necessarily mean you are bringing VALUE to what you are doing. Toooo busy should mean: not as effective, too much on the plate. Is your BUSY EFFECTIVE?!!?

REFLECTION

What stands out to me in this Reflection? What do I need to Change to Live this Fully? How will I Live this Today?

MARCH 11

Life is a Journey. Don't just focus on the end result! It is the PROCESS of the journey that holds the LESSONS that get you to the end.

REFLECTION

What stands out to me in this Reflection? What do I need to Change to Live this Fully? How will I Live this Today?

MARCH 12

Who you ARE is suppose to impact those who are in your realm of influence.
When you BECOME everything everyone else wants you to be, at the expense of
yourself, you become EMPTY AND STAGNANT. You are not tapping into the
GREATNESS that is already on the inside of you.
GOD designed you so you can flourish.

REFLECTION

What stands out to me in this Reflection? What do I need to Change to Live this Fully? How will I Live this Today?

MARCH 13

It is so fascinating to me that people get mad at YOU for something THEY did wrong. Don't carry other people's "stuff". Stay FREE. Don't let them "create" a atmosphere of guilt in YOU because they don't want to accept their issue.
STAY FREE.

REFLECTION

What stands out to me in this Reflection? What do I need to Change to Live this Fully? How will I Live this Today?

MARCH 14

Yes, people's WORD is suppose to be their BOND, but everyone is NOT "mature" enough (integrity) to live this out. Make sure that the people who give you their WORD values commitment as much as you do, especially if you are depending on them for something important.

REFLECTION

What stands out to me in this Reflection? What do I need to Change to Live this Fully? How will I Live this Today?

MARCH 15

Be mindful putting ALL your reliance on other people to accomplish your goals (even if they say they will). Make sure you follow up and always have a backup plan or you will find yourself disappointed.

REFLECTION

What stands out to me in this Reflection? What do I need to Change to Live this Fully? How will I Live this Today?

MARCH 16

Just because your "path" to the goal is not working out doesn't mean there is something wrong with the GOAL. The path can be "adjusted". There is more than one way to get to where you are going.

REFLECTION

What stands out to me in this Reflection? What do I need to Change to Live this Fully? How will I Live this Today?

MARCH 17

Just because it is difficult doesn't mean it's the devil. Just because it is easy doesn't mean it is God. Stay focused on the goal and make sure where you are going lines up with your directive not your circumstances.

REFLECTION

What stands out to me in this Reflection? What do I need to Change to Live this Fully? How will I Live this Today?

MARCH 18

A person without HOPE (expectation for better) is a person without DIRECTION and will remain STUCK in the midst of their circumstance because they do not have the "heart condition" necessary to MOVE FORWARD. They DWELL on what isn't instead of what CAN BE

REFLECTION

What stands out to me in this Reflection? What do I need to Change to Live this Fully? How will I Live this Today?

MARCH 19

Being OFFENDED doesn't make what was said less true. Offense just keeps you from seeing and acknowledging what you don't want to hear. You look for ways to "discredit" the one who said it by "looking" for THEIR issues. It is how you can justify IGNORING what was said, instead of asking YOURSELF
if what was said TRUE.

REFLECTION

What stands out to me in this Reflection? What do I need to Change to Live this Fully? How will I Live this Today?

MARCH 20

You need to learn to be o.k. with people not liking you. I know you are wonderful but everyone won't think so. So, stop trying to figure it out. Walk in peace. Don't let that become a distraction. Don't try to "convince" them otherwise.
Press forward.

REFLECTION

What stands out to me in this Reflection? What do I need to Change to Live this Fully? How will I Live this Today?

MARCH 21

Everyone is not going to agree with you.
Stand your ground regarding what you believe.

REFLECTION

What stands out to me in this Reflection? What do I need to Change to Live this Fully? How will I Live this Today?

Your WORD is a representation of your integrity and character. DO what you say you are going to do. If you are not going to do it, be woman enough to say so. Leaving people hanging to "guess" that your lack of action and/or ABSENCE IS the response is wrong.

REFLECTION

What stands out to me in this Reflection? What do I need to Change to Live this Fully? How will I Live this Today?

MARCH 23

Do not substitute how YOU see yourself with other people's opinion.
Self ACCEPTANCE is the beginning of healthy SELF ESTEEM

REFLECTION

What stands out to me in this Reflection? What do I need to Change to Live this Fully? How will I Live this Today?

MARCH 24

You tend to fear other people's opinion when you are INSECURE about your OWN opinion of the situation. You MUST release the fear of judgment; it keeps you from moving forward. Everyone is NOT going to agree with your decisions. That includes people you respect and love.

REFLECTION

What stands out to me in this Reflection? What do I need to Change to Live this Fully? How will I Live this Today?

MARCH 25

Just because you love and support someone does not mean you don't hold them to a standard of conduct (respect) in your relationship.
It is that RESPECT that undergirds and creates a healthy relationship

REFLECTION

What stands out to me in this Reflection? What do I need to Change to Live this Fully? How will I Live this Today?

MARCH 26

You CAN miss opportunities to INCREASE and LIVE a more fulfilling life when you DENY your part in making it better.

REFLECTION

What stands out to me in this Reflection? What do I need to Change to Live this Fully? How will I Live this Today?

MARCH 27

Walking by faith does not mean that you "ignore or deny" the issues you are responsible to handle. Faith is NOT the absence of responsibility.

REFLECTION

What stands out to me in this Reflection? What do I need to Change to Live this Fully? How will I Live this Today?

MARCH 28

Be QUICK to get over being angry when the issue is resolved.
Why continue to "run" the issue in the ground? Learn to move on.

REFLECTION

What stands out to me in this Reflection? What do I need to Change to Live this Fully? How will I Live this Today?

MARCH 29

Some things you NEED to hear won't feel good. They might make you mad.
Don't dismiss it because it makes you uncomfortable.

REFLECTION

What stands out to me in this Reflection? What do I need to Change to Live this Fully? How will I Live this Today?

MARCH 30

Give yourself permission to LIVE! You are putting limits on your life that keeps you from moving forward. YES, there will be challenges. Things in your life will need to be arranged, but that will be the CASE with or without your current circumstances. LIVE!

REFLECTION

What stands out to me in this Reflection? What do I need to Change to Live this Fully? How will I Live this Today?

MARCH 31

Why are you giving people space in your THOUGHT LIFE that don't matter? They don't like you. They mean you no good, but you continue to talk and think about them. STOP giving them valuable THOUGHT SPACE. Move forward.

REFLECTION

What stands out to me in this Reflection? What do I need to Change to Live this Fully? How will I Live this Today?

APRIL 1

Tearing someone else down doesn't make you more relevant or valuable. It doesn't solve your problem. It "elevates" YOUR "baggage" to the people you are talking to.

REFLECTION

What stands out to me in this Reflection? What do I need to Change to Live this Fully? How will I Live this Today?

APRIL 2

You have ONE life. When are you going to POSITION yourself and begin to LIVE and not just exist. Sometimes we act like we have a long time but we don't. The TIME is NOW!!
Don't leave the earth with your PURPOSE unfulfilled.

REFLECTION

What stands out to me in this Reflection? What do I need to Change to Live this Fully? How will I Live this Today?

APRIL 3

If you want a man of SUBSTANCE, you have to be a woman of SUBSTANCE. Just like you don't want a "jack leg brother", Men don't want anyone like that either. You want him to have a six pack, rich, great car, and money but you HAVE NOTHING to bring to the table. My PRECIOUS sister, he wants QUALITY TOO! What do you bring to the TABLE?!?

REFLECTION

What stands out to me in this Reflection? What do I need to Change to Live this Fully? How will I Live this Today?

APRIL 4

Are you wanting him so bad that you are willing to COMPROMISE WHO YOU ARE? Who you are is WHY he should want to be with you. If you give THAT UP, what's left? You are NO LONGER WHO attracted him in the first place.

REFLECTION

What stands out to me in this Reflection? What do I need to Change to Live this Fully? How will I Live this Today?

APRIL 5

SLOW DOWN. Stop rushing through "life" and "decisions". PROCESS. Think it through don't just RELY on what you "always" do. Maybe this time, something else needs to be done.

REFLECTION

What stands out to me in this Reflection? What do I need to Change to Live this Fully? How will I Live this Today?

APRIL 6

You are wondering WHY you won't do the things you SHOULD to change? It's because your EXCUSES are STILL greater than your REASON to DO something different.

REFLECTION
What stands out to me in this Reflection? What do I need to Change to Live this Fully? How will I Live this Today?

APRIL 7

Some "lessons" must be learned to "position" you for where you are going. If you find yourself going in circles STOP and say, "WHAT IS THE LESSON I AM SUPPOSE TO BE LEARNING?"

REFLECTION

What stands out to me in this Reflection? What do I need to Change to Live this Fully? How will I Live this Today?

APRIL 8

You live unnecessarily BENEATH your privilege when you don't have the knowledge to do better especially when it is available. You must take the TIME to get it.

REFLECTION

What stands out to me in this Reflection? What do I need to Change to Live this Fully? How will I Live this Today?

APRIL 9

Your mindset will either SUPPORT or UNDERMINE your goal.
Pay attention to what you are thinking.

REFLECTION

What stands out to me in this Reflection? What do I need to Change to Live this Fully? How will I Live this Today?

APRIL 10

Some things are "intentionally" not convenient. There is a lesson connected to YOU moving BEYOND the easy action so you are prepared for your next level. Check what you are avoiding or being "lazy" about. You just MIGHT be holding up your OWN stuff. hummmm.

REFLECTION

What stands out to me in this Reflection? What do I need to Change to Live this Fully? How will I Live this Today?

APRIL 11

CHECK your ATTITUDE. It is a REFLECTION of your view of the world and will impact what is AVAILABLE to you. Are you sarcastic or positive? Suspicious or Trusting? Pessimistic or Optimistic? Positive or Negative? Nasty or easy to get along? Needy or Independent?

REFLECTION

What stands out to me in this Reflection? What do I need to Change to Live this Fully? How will I Live this Today?

APRIL 12

When you are POSITIONED for greater you understand that:
It is a decision not a feeling. It is a discipline not something you fall into. It is developed not handed to you. It is pursued not given. It is available but must be desired. It is powerful but not forced. It will grow but must be activated.
Are you READY?

REFLECTION

What stands out to me in this Reflection? What do I need to Change to Live this Fully? How will I Live this Today?

APRIL 13

Without PROPER conditions you will be unfruitful. You will desire the right things but you will be unable to produce. What environment are you TRYING to grow in? Check your relationships, knowledge, habits, and location. Is it conducive to growth, stagnation or temporary evidence?

REFLECTION

What stands out to me in this Reflection? What do I need to Change to Live this Fully? How will I Live this Today?

APRIL 14

Whatever you've done to GET there, you will have to do to STAY.   If you plan on a permanent change and not just a temporary "fix" plan wisely and make sure you are willing to keep it up!

REFLECTION

What stands out to me in this Reflection? What do I need to Change to Live this Fully? How will I Live this Today?

APRIL 15

It's the small pieces that come TOGETHER to form the BIG picture. Don't "despise" the small beginnings. EMBRACE them because they are NECESSARY.

REFLECTION

What stands out to me in this Reflection? What do I need to Change to Live this Fully? How will I Live this Today?

APRIL 16

BEGIN where you are. DO what you have the ability to do NOW. Don't let what
you can't do DISTRACT and stop you from what you CAN.
Get focused and MOVE.

REFLECTION

What stands out to me in this Reflection? What do I need to Change to Live this Fully? How will I Live this Today?

APRIL 17

Have a protective attitude about who and what you allow in your personal space. Don't take that lightly. It DOES matter.

REFLECTION

What stands out to me in this Reflection? What do I need to Change to Live this Fully? How will I Live this Today?

APRIL 18

Just because you "don't know" what or how to fulfill your purpose, doesn't get you "off the hook" with God. It is your responsibility to POSITION yourself to find out and FULFILL it.

REFLECTION

What stands out to me in this Reflection? What do I need to Change to Live this Fully? How will I Live this Today?

APRIL 19

Your WHY for doing something has to be GREATER than your BEST excuses not to do it.

REFLECTION

What stands out to me in this Reflection? What do I need to Change to Live this Fully? How will I Live this Today?

APRIL 20

You CAN'T "die" without FULFILLING your purpose. What are you suppose to be doing? Life is GREATER than "bills and work". Dr. Munroe's death gave me a "aha" regarding this. He LIVED his life FULFILLING and he also FULFILLED many assignments that God had placed at his hand. I believe he died "empty" and without regret. If you died today what would be your regret? It is sooooooo NOT an OPTION. We must POSITION ourselves so we can see it!!

REFLECTION

What stands out to me in this Reflection? What do I need to Change to Live this Fully? How will I Live this Today?

APRIL 21

You don't change our ACTION until you increase
our knowledge and understanding.

REFLECTION

What stands out to me in this Reflection? What do I need to Change to Live this Fully? How will I Live this Today?

APRIL 22

STOP wishing for someone else to change in order to change your circumstance. They STILL have to make a decision for "themselves" not for you. It doesn't last if it is about YOU. What if they choose NOT to change? Then what? POSITION yourself for the change you seek for your life. "Wishing" for someone else to do something else is not a solution.

REFLECTION

What stands out to me in this Reflection? What do I need to Change to Live this Fully? How will I Live this Today?

APRIL 23

There is something that you need to do to "turn the page" for what is coming. Even Jesus had to "face the cross" to turn the page. What is it that you need to do? Yes you want to avoid it but like Christ in the Garden, the END RESULT is the focus, not the temporary experience of the moment. You need to 1. FOCUS on WHY you are doing it, 2. make the decision 3. and TURN THE PAGE.

REFLECTION

What stands out to me in this Reflection? What do I need to Change to Live this Fully? How will I Live this Today?

APRIL 24

KNOWLEDGE is one of the greatest gifts you can give yourself. We MUST train ourselves to DESIRE and SEEK it out. It is a game-changer.

REFLECTION

What stands out to me in this Reflection? What do I need to Change to Live this Fully? How will I Live this Today?

APRIL 25

Close down "voices" that go contrary to your purpose. You are in another season. What worked for you in the past is not designed for you next level, it just got you to it. You need to learn more.

REFLECTION

What stands out to me in this Reflection? What do I need to Change to Live this Fully? How will I Live this Today?

APRIL 26

TRANSITION isn't easy. You are being DEVELOPED and CHANGED. Like the butterfly, your whole system has to CHANGE and then BREAKOUT of the SHELL (the remains of who you USE to be). The results are AWESOME. Just like the butterfly PRESS, WIGGLE, STRETCH and DON'T GIVE UP. You are almost there.

REFLECTION

What stands out to me in this Reflection? What do I need to Change to Live this Fully? How will I Live this Today?

APRIL 27

You are a Unique Original. Don't devalue yourself being satisfied as a copy of someone you admire. The same wonder that God made them with, He made you. DISCOVER your Beautiful Wonder.

REFLECTION

What stands out to me in this Reflection? What do I need to Change to Live this Fully? How will I Live this Today?

APRIL 28

You can DESIRE to do something all day. But, DESIRE is just the beginning. You need ACTION to see "what" you desire come to pass. It will not happen on its own

REFLECTION

What stands out to me in this Reflection? What do I need to Change to Live this Fully? How will I Live this Today?

APRIL 29

It's easier to hold on to (people, jobs, mindset, organizations, routines, churches) because it is the "easy, safe, PREDICTABLE" thing to do. But when you are "miserable" or KNOW you should be doing something different and you STILL choose not to investigate and "discover" another path, you are doing yourself a disservice. Don't blame the people around you. You are the one who should move and decided not to. They are not the problem, it's your "fear" of coming out of the comfort of familiarity that is the issue.

REFLECTION

What stands out to me in this Reflection? What do I need to Change to Live this Fully? How will I Live this Today?

APRIL 30

Don't settle for what you know is NOT your destined end! You shouldn't RUSH into things and relationships "compromising" because you are scared you are going to miss something. 1. STOP and evaluate your situation 2. Be open to other possibilities 3. When you don't have "peace" (I am not talking about fear) don't move. TRUST your heart.

REFLECTION

What stands out to me in this Reflection? What do I need to Change to Live this Fully? How will I Live this Today?

MAY 1

Don't allow your dysfunction to become your normal function
because you have been doing it so long you no longer notice
that it is wrong.

REFLECTION

What stands out to me in this Reflection? What do I need to Change to Live this Fully? How will I Live this Today?

Don't ASSUME that people understand you are going to do something different, because you didn't SHOW UP or do what you said. You can NOT continue to be BLESSED living like that. If something CHANGES, say something. Don't just move on like you didn't have a conversation. Put on your big girl PANTIES so you can move your life forward and keep your "integrity" before people.

REFLECTION

What stands out to me in this Reflection? What do I need to Change to Live this Fully? How will I Live this Today?

MAY 3

We can be quick to "judge" another person's "baggage" when we don't take the time to REFLECT on our own. When you intentionally look at yourself and how hard it is for YOU to "work on" your OWN baggage, you are less likely to condemn. You will likely be slow to speak and show compassion. Why? You understand your own journey.

REFLECTION

What stands out to me in this Reflection? What do I need to Change to Live this Fully? How will I Live this Today?

Procrastination is AVOIDANCE. Ask yourself what are you avoiding and why? UNTIL you know and deal with it, the issue will not be solved and the action that you need to take won't get done. The main end result is regret.

REFLECTION

What stands out to me in this Reflection? What do I need to Change to Live this Fully? How will I Live this Today?

MAY 5

Be Careful consciously or unconsciously saying "I'll be happy when....." and then "waiting" for this "special time" to come so you can be happy. Circumstances DON'T have to control your emotions or perspective. CHOOSE to be Happy in spite of.

REFLECTION
What stands out to me in this Reflection? What do I need to Change to Live this Fully? How will I Live this Today?

MAY 6

Make up your mind to SHIFT. Certain things won't manifest until you are "ALL IN". You go back and forth because you are not CONVINCED. Settle it by solving the excuses that keep you from committing! 1. Understand that the season for "that" is over. 2. Begin to get EXCITED about laying the groundwork for this new season. 3. Know that every new season has new information, truths and wisdom you must LEARN to support what you will experience and what you need to be successful.

REFLECTION

What stands out to me in this Reflection? What do I need to Change to Live this Fully? How will I Live this Today?

Hold on to your HOPES and DREAMS. It is not SELFISH to want to fulfill the PURPOSE you feel in your heart. Yes, you have responsibilities. Yes, you have roles in other people's lives. But that doesn't NEGATE the PURPOSE you were created to fulfill.

REFLECTION

What stands out to me in this Reflection? What do I need to Change to Live this Fully? How will I Live this Today?

MAY 8

In the movies, you see someone in the middle of a situation and they LAUGH! You say to yourself, how do they laugh in the midst of that. When you laugh OUT LOUD you are reminding yourself and your enemy, YOU AIN"T OUT YET!!!. Remember, 1. don't take "everything" so serious to the point that it steals your peace (even some of the hard things), 2. Learn to LAUGH, It is a "sign" to yourself and the enemy. that IN SPITE of you WILL win.

REFLECTION

What stands out to me in this Reflection? What do I need to Change to Live this Fully? How will I Live this Today?

MAY 9

Take the time to recharge your spirit, soul, and body. You cannot continuously remain on go and never make time to refuel, and expect to function normally. Learn to do whatever is necessary to ensure proper functionality. Stop putting it off. Your life, family, business, and goals will thank you.

REFLECTION

What stands out to me in this Reflection? What do I need to Change to Live this Fully? How will I Live this Today?

MAY 10

When you work on your purpose you don't have time to focus on other people.

REFLECTION

What stands out to me in this Reflection? What do I need to Change to Live this Fully? How will I Live this Today?

MAY 11

Your emotions JOB is to "support" your decisions, NOT make them. If you are EMOTIONAL about a situation, a DECISION, perspective or assumption has ALREADY been made.

REFLECTION

What stands out to me in this Reflection? What do I need to Change to Live this Fully? How will I Live this Today?

MAY 12

STOP "scheduling" your Destiny and Goals around your friends! The majority of them ain't gonna go with you (they just talking) and the majority of them are NOT gonna buy from you. (Its just the truth). DECIDE to DO YOU and Move FORWARD.

REFLECTION

What stands out to me in this Reflection? What do I need to Change to Live this Fully? How will I Live this Today?

MAY 13

A lot of times we get a "high" off a good idea but never intend to implement it. We get in the habit of the "idea buzz". It's now TIME to implement and do what you need to do to see the manifestation of your vision. Don't let the "idea buzz" REPLACE true implementation.

REFLECTION

What stands out to me in this Reflection? What do I need to Change to Live this Fully? How will I Live this Today?

MAY 14

We can't allow the COMFORT of old habits to DICTATE our NEW and necessary ACTIONS or even the BEST INTENTIONS will be defeated.

REFLECTION

What stands out to me in this Reflection? What do I need to Change to Live this Fully? How will I Live this Today?

MAY 15

Be careful letting your CURRENT circumstance "limit" your thinking and you REDUCE your VISION for your FUTURE! Your future is the BLUEPRINT that guides you

REFLECTION

What stands out to me in this Reflection? What do I need to Change to Live this Fully? How will I Live this Today?

MAY 16

Break down your goals into small pieces. Even if you go minute by minute. Those minutes turn into hours and those hours turn into days. TAKE the NEXT STEP. Don't just focus so hard on the big picture. It is there. If you go step by step, you will look UP and have accomplished the goal

REFLECTION

What stands out to me in this Reflection? What do I need to Change to Live this Fully? How will I Live this Today?

MAY 17

Miserable people want to make you miserable.
Be mindful giving them "energy or relevance" with your attention.

REFLECTION

What stands out to me in this Reflection? What do I need to Change to Live this Fully? How will I Live this Today?

MAY 18

HARD TRUTH: Don't let the people who "walk away" from you devastate you. REMEMBER the majority of people make choices that benefit them FIRST, before if benefits you. Apparently they couldn't satisfy you and THEM. It's THEIR LOSS. Let them go.

REFLECTION

What stands out to me in this Reflection? What do I need to Change to Live this Fully? How will I Live this Today?

MAY 19

REFUSE to let complaining feel good or satisfying to your ego/flesh. REFUSE to let it be your "first" reaction to conflict. REFUSE to let the negativity "run" through your thoughts. INSTEAD of complaining, DETERMINE to solve the issue.

REFLECTION

What stands out to me in this Reflection? What do I need to Change to Live this Fully? How will I Live this Today?

MAY 20

You CAN begin again!! Age is just a number. NO, your time has not run out! NO, you are not "stuck" and unable to do something else. There is STILL much for you to do. Your MINDSET determines what is available to you. Make up you mind and BECOME who you are meant to be

REFLECTION

What stands out to me in this Reflection? What do I need to Change to Live this Fully? How will I Live this Today?

MAY 21

If you allow it, FEAR will cause you to talk YOURSELF out of your Destiny. Remember, Fears job is not to stop you. Fears job is to make you stop YOURSELF. Why? So you will get so focused on NOT doing what you should, that you lose heart and won't PROCEED in spite of what has happened. DUST yourself off and stop listening to FEAR and LISTEN to your DESTINY!!!

REFLECTION

What stands out to me in this Reflection? What do I need to Change to Live this Fully? How will I Live this Today?

MAY 22

Miserable people want to make others miserable.
Be mindful giving them energy or relevance with your attention.

REFLECTION

What stands out to me in this Reflection? What do I need to Change to Live this Fully? How will I Live this Today?

MAY 23

Don't SETTLE. Yes, life happens and it CAN "wear you down". You find yourself wanting to stop "fighting" and you are tired. THEN you start thinking about SETTLING and trying to convince yourself that it is best. Don't do it. You KNOW there is more. You are worth it and so is your future. EXPECT great things

REFLECTION

What stands out to me in this Reflection? What do I need to Change to Live this Fully? How will I Live this Today?

MAY 24

Don't let CHALLENGES back you up and then you say, "Well maybe it wasn't meant to be." It IS MEANT to BE. Some things you WILL have to STAND and fight to make happen. Make the DECISION to STAND and FIGHT. Go get your stuff! .

REFLECTION

What stands out to me in this Reflection? What do I need to Change to Live this Fully? How will I Live this Today?

MAY 25

NO is not a dirty word. Saying it doesn't "make" you selfish. You can say NO even if you DON'T have something else to do. STOP overpacking your schedule and life and then complain about it. Just say NO..... you can do it. Don't explain why. Let's PRACTICE.... No.

REFLECTION

What stands out to me in this Reflection? What do I need to Change to Live this Fully? How will I Live this Today?

MAY 26

People will ALWAYS have something to say about what they know NOTHING about.

REFLECTION

What stands out to me in this Reflection? What do I need to Change to Live this Fully? How will I Live this Today?

MAY 27

Loving yourself BEGINS with accepting who you are TODAY (good and bad), NOT waiting to get to who you would prefer to be.

REFLECTION

What stands out to me in this Reflection? What do I need to Change to Live this Fully? How will I Live this Today?

MAY 28

To many times we ASSUME we can't have something and just move on. We never ASK, INQUIRE, or have a alternative to GET what we want. If you don't ask, you could MISS OUT on what was for you. Everyone is not going to just "offer". Stop dwelling on the possible "rejection" and STAND on the possible "ACCEPTANCE". Change your mindset

REFLECTION

What stands out to me in this Reflection? What do I need to Change to Live this Fully? How will I Live this Today?

MAY 29

We have all experienced DELAYs in our lives. Sometimes, things don't happen "when" we expect them 2. We must be careful not to "pre-categorize" these DELAYs as DEAD ENDS and QUIT or dismiss it because it's not what we expected. Be "open" to other ways of getting to where your going. Don't get STUCK in a "certain" way and ONLY way mindset.

REFLECTION

What stands out to me in this Reflection? What do I need to Change to Live this Fully? How will I Live this Today?

MAY 30

You must do the INNER/SELF work and positioning to "support" the Vision that is in your heart. Yes, God has a part, but He is partnering with YOU for YOUR purpose. You are VITAL to its success. Without YOU it won't work. God doesn't do it for you or by himself.

REFLECTION

What stands out to me in this Reflection? What do I need to Change to Live this Fully? How will I Live this Today?

MAY 31

Focus on the goal. Challenges are a part of the equation. Don't let it shut you down. FIND the solution and keep it moving.

REFLECTION

What stands out to me in this Reflection? What do I need to Change to Live this Fully? How will I Live this Today?

JUNE 1

SUBDUE your thought life. One of the roots of SELF SABOTAGE is your perspective. You allow thoughts like: I cant, not enough, not as good, can't do like that, not as pretty, she is better, I don't have the skills. What you DWELL on GROWS! Think on what you WANT.

REFLECTION

What stands out to me in this Reflection? What do I need to Change to Live this Fully? How will I Live this Today?

JUNE 2

YOU ARE ENOUGH!!! God did not give you "LESS" than someone else. You just have something "different" and it is that difference that makes you UNIQUE and VALUABLE. It is up to YOU to "WORK IT"!!! How you "interpret". "develop" and "leverage" what you have will determine YOUR outcome.

REFLECTION

What stands out to me in this Reflection? What do I need to Change to Live this Fully? How will I Live this Today?

JUNE 3

Your LIFE is a "reflection" of the beliefs you have allowed to GUIDE your decisions. Analyze the beliefs of your ACTIONS not just the one's you are speaking. It is the beliefs of your ACTIONS that show the truth of your heart.

REFLECTION

What stands out to me in this Reflection? What do I need to Change to Live this Fully? How will I Live this Today?

JUNE 4

People make DECISIONS and plans around what YOU say you can do. 1. Don't just walk away as if you didn't say anything 2. Don't wait till the last minute to change your mind. 3. Don't "pretend" you never made the commitment and let the "commitment" date pass and pretend you forgot. 4. Hold to your word. 5. Don't make commitments you can't keep trying to impress people. 6. Make every effort to keep your word, even if it is inconvenient. YOUR WORD MATTERS. It is a reflection of you!!

REFLECTION

What stands out to me in this Reflection? What do I need to Change to Live this Fully? How will I Live this Today?

JUNE 5

You really don't realize what you have been MISSING until you do something different. Refuse to be comfortable "living" with DYSFUNCTION as your norm. CHASE after the BEST and don't "settle". You don't have to.

REFLECTION

What stands out to me in this Reflection? What do I need to Change to Live this Fully? How will I Live this Today?

JUNE 6

Be careful not to let the "failures" of your past, be the "excuses" for not moving forward towards your future. You can BEGIN AGAIN. You didn't miss your season, JUST a opportunity. There will be other opportunities

REFLECTION

What stands out to me in this Reflection? What do I need to Change to Live this Fully? How will I Live this Today?

JUNE 7

It is easier to TELL people what to do, rather than EMPOWER them to make their own choices. BUT, you do them a disservice. You create a dependency that is not to their advantage. Choose to empower

REFLECTION

What stands out to me in this Reflection? What do I need to Change to Live this Fully? How will I Live this Today?

JUNE 8

Be careful giving advice. Just because YOU would handle it a certain way, doesn't mean others should. Be a SUPPORT. Being a support doesn't mean you "agree" with their choice, but make sure you don't "LIVE" your opinion through others

REFLECTION

What stands out to me in this Reflection? What do I need to Change to Live this Fully? How will I Live this Today?

JUNE 9

You can't control people's perception of you. Be yourself and those who WANT to "really" know the TRUTH will get to know you themselves.

REFLECTION

What stands out to me in this Reflection? What do I need to Change to Live this Fully? How will I Live this Today?

JUNE 10

Everyone has an opinion and not all will agree with yours. 1. Stop letting people "guilt bully" you into what they believe. 2. Learn to stand for your opinion. 3. Learn to listen and have a intelligent conversation whether you agree or not. That is how we learn from one another..... exchange not isolation.

REFLECTION

What stands out to me in this Reflection? What do I need to Change to Live this Fully? How will I Live this Today?

JUNE 11

EMBRACE becoming the "GREATEST EXPRESSION" of who you are. As you embrace the journey, the greatness God placed in you to fulfill your Life DESTINY and PURPOSE will be released!

REFLECTION

What stands out to me in this Reflection? What do I need to Change to Live this Fully? How will I Live this Today?

JUNE 12

The areas in your life that you fail to work on, END UP being the areas you need for your next season. Don't put off doing what needs to be done in this season. NOW is preparation for what is to come

REFLECTION

What stands out to me in this Reflection? What do I need to Change to Live this Fully? How will I Live this Today?

JUNE 13

YOU are not what you DO. What you DO is suppose to be a avenue of "expression" because of WHO you are. The situation for most is we had to deal with responsibilities before we "knew" ourselves and we allowed those "responsibilities" to define us. It is time to develop your IDENTITY so you can LIVE fulfilled and in alignment with the purpose you were created to fulfill.

REFLECTION

What stands out to me in this Reflection? What do I need to Change to Live this Fully? How will I Live this Today?

JUNE 14

Becoming who you are "meant" to be is NOT a option. It is your destiny. We must STEP INTO the journey of BECOMING, so we can fulfill our purpose. Make up your mind to begin.

REFLECTION

What stands out to me in this Reflection? What do I need to Change to Live this Fully? How will I Live this Today?

JUNE 15

We can get so "caught up" in the negative things going on in our lives that we don't even SEE the good. There is something in your life that you can appreciate, FIND IT and let it bring LIFE to you. As the word says, "think on THESE things"

REFLECTION

What stands out to me in this Reflection? What do I need to Change to Live this Fully? How will I Live this Today?

JUNE 16

Your WORDS do matter. What you say DOES have a impact. Be mindful what you speak over your circumstance. Pay attention to your conversation. Does it "support" where you are going. Have you allowed it to be to "loose"?

REFLECTION

What stands out to me in this Reflection? What do I need to Change to Live this Fully? How will I Live this Today?

JUNE 17

If you KNOW you are suppose to "turn left"... "turn left". STOP looking at the "benefits" of turning right. You're INVITING doubt into your circumstance.

REFLECTION

What stands out to me in this Reflection? What do I need to Change to Live this Fully? How will I Live this Today?

JUNE 18

You do not have to get MAD when people don't agree with your opinion

REFLECTION

What stands out to me in this Reflection? What do I need to Change to Live this Fully? How will I Live this Today?

JUNE 19

I found a baby tree growing in my flower bed. Is it harming it? No. BUT it doesn't belong and eventually it will harm my flower bed. Its the same in our lives. There are people, habits, circumstances that IN THE MOMENT, don't "seem" to harm, but eventually it will. Pull it up NOW, don't wait till its "roots" are deep

REFLECTION

What stands out to me in this Reflection? What do I need to Change to Live this Fully? How will I Live this Today?

JUNE 20

I am sorry I have to say this, but for some of you... your FRIENDS will NOT be your GREATEST SUPPORTERS. STOP being shocked!! We fail to realize that relationships are built on being "common/same" with one another. So, If you are doing something that no longer makes you "common/same" to them, MORE than likely they will not support it. Don't get MAD. Find the people who support where you are going

REFLECTION

What stands out to me in this Reflection? What do I need to Change to Live this Fully? How will I Live this Today?

JUNE 21

YOU are your best competition. Working to become the GREATEST EXPRESSION of yourself leaves no time to look at someone else.

REFLECTION

What stands out to me in this Reflection? What do I need to Change to Live this Fully? How will I Live this Today?

JUNE 22

Married Ladies, your husband does NOT complete you. You are already WHOLE, and if you are not work on YOU for you NOT because you are married . DON'T loose your IDENTITY because you have a "man" in your life. Live your life NOW. Find YOUR passion NOW. Discover and do what you like NOW. Have friends NOW. Dress great for YOU NOW. LIVE!!!

REFLECTION

What stands out to me in this Reflection? What do I need to Change to Live this Fully? How will I Live this Today?

JUNE 23

Don't let people "bait" you into a argument. A lot of times they do it to "set up and justify" what they want to do AFTER THE FIGHT. Don't give them the ammo. It usually happens when you feel it necessary to defend yourself. Why defend yourself about stupidity? When you KNOW the truth there is nothing to defend.

REFLECTION

What stands out to me in this Reflection? What do I need to Change to Live this Fully? How will I Live this Today?

JUNE 24

Be wary of people in leadership who don't want you to THINK or ask questions and just want you to "obey"

REFLECTION

What stands out to me in this Reflection? What do I need to Change to Live this Fully? How will I Live this Today?

JUNE 25

Sometimes it's not THAT you said it, it's HOW you said it.

REFLECTION

What stands out to me in this Reflection? What do I need to Change to Live this Fully? How will I Live this Today?

JUNE 26

When you can't be corrected you can't grow

REFLECTION

What stands out to me in this Reflection? What do I need to Change to Live this Fully? How will I Live this Today?

JUNE 27

Ask for help. STOP wasting time trying to figure out what someone has already walked out. Don't let your ego tell you they will think less of you. A person who HAS WALKED where you are going understands the journey! So, they have a genuine and sincere desire to see you succeed. They've been there.

REFLECTION

What stands out to me in this Reflection? What do I need to Change to Live this Fully? How will I Live this Today?

JUNE 28

STOP talking like ALLLLL women are caddy, backbiting, evil, and hateful and you "just don't do women". There are AWESOME, POWERFUL, KIND, FAITHFUL, SINCERE and LOVING women out there. When you "close yourself off" you will NEVER see the ones you NEED. OH YES, you need us! There is wisdom, grace, perspective, knowledge and understanding that WE can ONLY give to each other.

REFLECTION

What stands out to me in this Reflection? What do I need to Change to Live this Fully? How will I Live this Today?

JUNE 29

We want God to give us SPECIFIC instructions but when He does... we talk ourselves out of the instructions. Learn to trust the instructions and do your part

REFLECTION

What stands out to me in this Reflection? What do I need to Change to Live this Fully? How will I Live this Today?

JUNE 30

If you NEVER get a "thank you..I appreciate you... you are special.. I couldn't do it without you", DON'T "devalue" yourself because people don't know how to appreciate you! Learn to ACKNOWLEDGE and appreciate yourself

REFLECTION

What stands out to me in this Reflection? What do I need to Change to Live this Fully? How will I Live this Today?

JULY 1

The longer it takes for you to walk in your purpose and speak your LIFE MESSAGE, the longer WE have to wait to be impacted by what ONLY you can give our lives. There is no REPLACEMENT or SUBSTITUTE for YOUR VOICE. You are holding up our STUFF. Let's GO!!! Let's BE about it.

REFLECTION

What stands out to me in this Reflection? What do I need to Change to Live this Fully? How will I Live this Today?

JULY 2

Our actions have consequences BEYOND the moment

REFLECTION

What stands out to me in this Reflection? What do I need to Change to Live this Fully? How will I Live this Today?

JULY 3

Be careful coming at people as if your "opinion" (interpretation) is the only one and call it your "spiritual responsibility" to correct. Be ready for a response and don't get mad when your "opinion" is not accepted.
Those that win souls MUST be wise

REFLECTION

What stands out to me in this Reflection? What do I need to Change to Live this Fully? How will I Live this Today?

JULY 4

How many signs do you NEED before you move. lolol. He has already given you 2 yes, a confirmation in church, a prophesy through the preacher on tv, a sign at the grocery store on the magazine cover, a tv commercial with the EXACT words you heard at church and a word through your child! It's on YOU Sweetie

REFLECTION

What stands out to me in this Reflection? What do I need to Change to Live this Fully? How will I Live this Today?

JULY 5

Your light is not meant to be dimmed it is meant to shine. When it shines it will "irritate" those who are comfortable in darkness but let your light so shine!! Don't dim your light to conform to darkness, people are suppose to conform to the light. SHINE!

REFLECTION

What stands out to me in this Reflection? What do I need to Change to Live this Fully? How will I Live this Today?

JULY 6

Don't loose your individuality because you are married

REFLECTION

What stands out to me in this Reflection? What do I need to Change to Live this Fully? How will I Live this Today?

JULY 7

Sometimes you have to buy your OWN flowers, dinner, vacation, or outfit. Love on your OWN self. You know what you deserve.

REFLECTION

What stands out to me in this Reflection? What do I need to Change to Live this Fully? How will I Live this Today?

JULY 8

Setting personal BOUNDARIES does NOT mean: 1. you are mean 2. you are not being Christian 3. you are not friendly or available. Setting boundaries is SHARING what you will and will not accept in your space. Where there are no boundaries, there is "abuse." Let people know where you stand! Don't get mad if you never told them what IS or IS NOT acceptable. It is HEALTHY and creates HEALTHY relationships. YOU teach people how to treat you

REFLECTION

What stands out to me in this Reflection? What do I need to Change to Live this Fully? How will I Live this Today?

JULY 9

We must LEARN to PRESS THRU! We MUST UNLEARN the BEHAVIOR of SHUT DOWN. There is no "progress" with this behavior. You will never EXPERIENCE the TASTE of VICTORY if you keep getting distracted. You will never DEVELOP the "NEVER GIVE UP" attitude if you don't make it to the end! NO MORE SHUTTING DOWN. PRESS THRU and you will experience the VICTORY on the other side!!!

REFLECTION

What stands out to me in this Reflection? What do I need to Change to Live this Fully? How will I Live this Today?

JULY 10

Stop putting yourself off. You are important 2

REFLECTION

What stands out to me in this Reflection? What do I need to Change to Live this Fully? How will I Live this Today?

JULY 11

As you move forward, some relationships will AUTOMATICALLY fall off. Yes, it will hurt, BUT the person that you ARE BECOMING no longer has anything in COMMON with them. It is o.k., remember the good times and
KEEP MOVING FORWARD.

REFLECTION

What stands out to me in this Reflection? What do I need to Change to Live this Fully? How will I Live this Today?

JULY 12

SPIRITUAL WARFARE is not just about talking in tongues. It is ALSO making up your MIND not to be MOVED by a situation that really hurts and STAYING strong because you KNOW that you will win

REFLECTION

What stands out to me in this Reflection? What do I need to Change to Live this Fully? How will I Live this Today?

JULY 13

STOP "attacking" people's relationship with God because they don't think or interpret "text" the same way you do

REFLECTION

What stands out to me in this Reflection? What do I need to Change to Live this Fully? How will I Live this Today?

JULY 14

When things get "overwhelming" slow down. Take the time to WRITE out what you need to do. It helps bring clarity and focus.

REFLECTION

What stands out to me in this Reflection? What do I need to Change to Live this Fully? How will I Live this Today?

JULY 15

Say it with me. "The pieces WILL come together."

REFLECTION

What stands out to me in this Reflection? What do I need to Change to Live this Fully? How will I Live this Today?

JULY 16

Don't "freeze" your life waiting for an apology. Whether you get it or not, YOU
are still responsible to move your life forward.
Stop giving away your power. LIVE.

REFLECTION

What stands out to me in this Reflection? What do I need to Change to Live this Fully? How will I Live this Today?

JULY 17

Growth is being able to handle effectively what use to be a stumbling block. Say it with me, "Im growing"

REFLECTION

What stands out to me in this Reflection? What do I need to Change to Live this Fully? How will I Live this Today?

JULY 18

Don't let "life" steal your LIFE.

REFLECTION

What stands out to me in this Reflection? What do I need to Change to Live this Fully? How will I Live this Today?

JULY 19

CAN I BE PLAIN? You acting depressed, looking bad, talking low and pitiful, and not doing things in front of them is "TOO MUCH WORK" to get someone to " acknowledge" they are wrong or to get them to ask you what's wrong. Say what you need to say. Stop throwing "hints" and move on.

REFLECTION

What stands out to me in this Reflection? What do I need to Change to Live this Fully? How will I Live this Today?

JULY 20

When people say " you think you all that?" .... you BETTA look them in the eye, smile and say Yessss! Don't let people try to make you put yourself down... confidence is NOT arrogance. Call them on it.

REFLECTION

What stands out to me in this Reflection? What do I need to Change to Live this Fully? How will I Live this Today?

JULY 21

You can't meet a Prince looking like a maid, even Cinderella had to change clothes to be recognized for who she really was!!!!

REFLECTION

What stands out to me in this Reflection? What do I need to Change to Live this Fully? How will I Live this Today?

JULY 22

Stop thinking that people should "think" like you. NO, they are NOT thinking that you are tired. NO, they are not going to do it because it is the "right thing to do". NO, they are not feeling guilty about letting you do everything. YOU set the boundaries for how people treat you. SET the boundaries

REFLECTION

What stands out to me in this Reflection? What do I need to Change to Live this Fully? How will I Live this Today?

JULY 23

Are you a supporter or a rescuer? A lot of times our "busy" is us taking on the responsibility of others instead of "supporting" others in THEIR responsibility.

REFLECTION

What stands out to me in this Reflection? What do I need to Change to Live this Fully? How will I Live this Today?

JULY 24

When you have a "call" on your life, you don't do what is "popular", you do what your MANDATE tells you to do! Popularity is not a DIRECTION.

REFLECTION

What stands out to me in this Reflection? What do I need to Change to Live this Fully? How will I Live this Today?

JULY 25

It's hard to move forward if you haven't decided where to go. You will look like you are moving but in the end you are just marching in place. Get focused.

REFLECTION

What stands out to me in this Reflection? What do I need to Change to Live this Fully? How will I Live this Today?

JULY 26

Be mindful if you give more "value" to other people's perspective/opinion and are quick to abandon your own. You can respect another perspective without loosing yours.

REFLECTION

What stands out to me in this Reflection? What do I need to Change to Live this Fully? How will I Live this Today?

JULY 27

Forgiveness is not saying someone didn't do something. It is "releasing" them from the responsibility to FIX it. You make the decision to move YOUR OWN life forward with or without their acknowledgement.

REFLECTION

What stands out to me in this Reflection? What do I need to Change to Live this Fully? How will I Live this Today?

JULY 28

SPEAK over your life (so your ears can hear). Don't just think over it. You need to hear YOUR declaration! SPEAK IT!

REFLECTION

What stands out to me in this Reflection? What do I need to Change to Live this Fully? How will I Live this Today?

JULY 29

The "aha moments" don't happen when you are trying to decide if you are GOING to jump, it happens after you JUMP!!.

REFLECTION

What stands out to me in this Reflection? What do I need to Change to Live this Fully? How will I Live this Today?

JULY 30

Challenges do NOT mean it will not come together.
Don't be so quick to give up or shut down.

REFLECTION

What stands out to me in this Reflection? What do I need to Change to Live this Fully? How will I Live this Today?

JULY 31

Don't let their "volume" convince you they are right when you KNOW you are.
Stop diminishing your "value" to the conversation because they "seem" confident.
Some people hide behind volume and words to disguise their insecurity or
ignorance. Learn to hold your ground and trust your heart!

REFLECTION

What stands out to me in this Reflection? What do I need to Change to Live this Fully? How will I Live this Today?

AUGUST 1

Time can be your friend or enemy depending on how you use it.

REFLECTION

What stands out to me in this Reflection? What do I need to Change to Live this Fully? How will I Live this Today?

AUGUST 2

Speak into someone else's life what you want spoken in yours.
If you want to be encouraged.... encourage.

REFLECTION

What stands out to me in this Reflection? What do I need to Change to Live this Fully? How will I Live this Today?

AUGUST 3

Be mindful teaching or giving "advice" about what you are not living or lived. Why? Because when the challenges come (they will) against the TRUTH you are sharing, and you haven't lived or had experience thru it, you won't have the most effective answers or encouragement for those you've taught...regarding those challenges that come. Then they are lost and you are guessing about what they should say or do. So, LIVE your truth.

REFLECTION

What stands out to me in this Reflection? What do I need to Change to Live this Fully? How will I Live this Today?

AUGUST 4

Fear will make you convince YOURSELF that "if you try" it won't work AND then you will search for people who agree. Stop rehearsing why it won't work and DECLARE why it will. GUESS WHAT?? There are people who will agree

REFLECTION

What stands out to me in this Reflection? What do I need to Change to Live this Fully? How will I Live this Today?

AUGUST 5

Discipline will open the door to your "next". Learning the "habits/lifestyle" of your "next" is also necessary to STAY there.

REFLECTION

What stands out to me in this Reflection? What do I need to Change to Live this Fully? How will I Live this Today?

AUGUST 6

Stop limiting yourself to the "four walls of the church". Everyone is not CALLED to do ministry there. There is a WORLD that needs to SEE God, not just the Christians in the building.

REFLECTION

What stands out to me in this Reflection? What do I need to Change to Live this Fully? How will I Live this Today?

AUGUST 7

Just because the MAJORITY is doing something doesn't mean it is right for you.
Don't be afraid to STAND alone.

REFLECTION

What stands out to me in this Reflection? What do I need to Change to Live this Fully? How will I Live this Today?

AUGUST 8

The "stronghold" you refuse/ignore when convenient, will be waiting for you in front of the opportunity you desire. It will need to be addressed and YOU will be inconvenienced. STOP putting it off.

REFLECTION

What stands out to me in this Reflection? What do I need to Change to Live this Fully? How will I Live this Today?

AUGUST 9

Be mindful "needing" to AFFIRM your "truth" by either getting AGREEMENT or DESTROYING someone else's in the name of "helping/sharing". Living your truth is really the GREATEST testimony of it.

REFLECTION

What stands out to me in this Reflection? What do I need to Change to Live this Fully? How will I Live this Today?

AUGUST 10

CHANGE is not convenient but it is necessary.
It will cost you something.

REFLECTION

What stands out to me in this Reflection? What do I need to Change to Live this Fully? How will I Live this Today?

AUGUST 11

A person who is Self Sufficient understands when to accept help. A person functioning in PRIDE says I don't need anyone! One has its roots in healthy independence and the other hurt and disappointment. Don't CONFUSE PRIDE with self sufficiency

REFLECTION

What stands out to me in this Reflection? What do I need to Change to Live this Fully? How will I Live this Today?

AUGUST 12

REMEMBER: What you compromise to GET, You will have to compromise to keep, because what you DID got you the results! Is it worth it? CHARACTER is vital in developing and "becoming" yourself in the "fullest" measure. CHARACTER is having CONSISTENT behavior that reflects your beliefs and values, no matter what is going on in your life. You won't compromise for the "moment" and then RETURN to "yourself". The fact that you come "out of character" indicates that you need to evaluate your "real" belief and values. You need to be honest with yourself and investigate your decision.

REFLECTION

What stands out to me in this Reflection? What do I need to Change to Live this Fully? How will I Live this Today?

AUGUST 13

A lot of times people are stuck because they "refuse" to get and activate the knowledge necessary to shift. They are looking to be "rescued" without the responsibility to change their behavior. They want to stay the same AND get what they want.

REFLECTION

What stands out to me in this Reflection? What do I need to Change to Live this Fully? How will I Live this Today?

AUGUST 14

When you ignore, pretend and put off things that need to be dealt with, it "cost" more to fix then if you would have addressed it when it arose. Stop putting it off.

REFLECTION

What stands out to me in this Reflection? What do I need to Change to Live this Fully? How will I Live this Today?

AUGUST 15

Your way is not the only way to get things done. "Allow" other people to have their opinion (children, husband, friends, etc.)

REFLECTION

What stands out to me in this Reflection? What do I need to Change to Live this Fully? How will I Live this Today?

AUGUST 16

Stop living in "burnout" and making it your norm. Learn to take the time to be restored, renewed and revived spirit, soul and body. It's not a option, it is a necessity

REFLECTION

What stands out to me in this Reflection? What do I need to Change to Live this Fully? How will I Live this Today?

AUGUST 17

Your success is on the other side of your excuse

REFLECTION

What stands out to me in this Reflection? What do I need to Change to Live this Fully? How will I Live this Today?

AUGUST 18

NO, you don't have to be "overwhelmed". Take things "off your plate" that don't belong to you. STOP doing everything for everyone, "thinking" you are the only one that can do things. RESET.

REFLECTION

What stands out to me in this Reflection? What do I need to Change to Live this Fully? How will I Live this Today?

AUGUST 19

Don't be ashamed to want MORE! Prosperity is the inheritance of the saints!
Poverty is NOT a positive reflection of the Kingdom

REFLECTION

What stands out to me in this Reflection? What do I need to Change to Live this Fully? How will I Live this Today?

AUGUST 20

Assumption should never be a substitute for communication.

REFLECTION

What stands out to me in this Reflection? What do I need to Change to Live this Fully? How will I Live this Today?

AUGUST 21

Be mindful what you "meditate" on. You are a product of what you think. Make sure your thoughts are a reflection of who you want to be. Anything that does not support how you see yourself, refuse to allow it in your thought life

REFLECTION

What stands out to me in this Reflection? What do I need to Change to Live this Fully? How will I Live this Today?

AUGUST 22

Speak what you want to manifest in your life. Take it out of your head and put it on your lips! You don't have to tell anyone, but YOU need to DECLARE it so.

REFLECTION

What stands out to me in this Reflection? What do I need to Change to Live this Fully? How will I Live this Today?

AUGUST 23

Do you RETALIATE when people tell you something about yourself you don't like? Do you hold a grudge and make them wish they would have never said anything? Do you walk in offense and think of ways to tell that person negatives about themselves? You need to "check" that! If you can't "hear" you are creating a very UNHEALTHY atmosphere for relationship that doesn't end well.

REFLECTION

What stands out to me in this Reflection? What do I need to Change to Live this Fully? How will I Live this Today?

AUGUST 24

REGRET is not a good friend. Don't allow it to take you down memory lane about what didn't, coulda, shoulda, woulda, if. The decisions have been made. NOW, its time to move forward. You CAN move forward irregardless of what has happened. MOVE! Possibilities are STILL before you. GREATER is STILL before you. INCREASE is STILL before you. No turning back.

REFLECTION

What stands out to me in this Reflection? What do I need to Change to Live this Fully? How will I Live this Today?

AUGUST 25

We all need people in our lives who accept us for who we are YET encouraging us to become our GREATER.

REFLECTION

What stands out to me in this Reflection? What do I need to Change to Live this Fully? How will I Live this Today?

AUGUST 26

STOP waiting for stuff to happen to you and go out and make it happen! A lot of what you are "waiting" on doesn't move till you do.

REFLECTION

What stands out to me in this Reflection? What do I need to Change to Live this Fully? How will I Live this Today?

AUGUST 27

EVERY season or level in your life has a LEARNING CURVE necessary for you to move and STAY in it. Some people don't think they need to GROW because they have the "ability" to START in the new. BUT, we are not talking about going IN, we are talking about STAYING. SEE, where you are now, opens the door but you don't just want to open the door YOU WANT TO STAY. So grow! Don't keep going through the SAME motions, falling backwards and thinking that it's the devil, or people keeping you from your destiny. YOU need more knowledge and maturity. People and the devil can't keep you from what God has ORDAINED for you. Look at you FIRST.

REFLECTION

What stands out to me in this Reflection? What do I need to Change to Live this Fully? How will I Live this Today?

AUGUST 28

Don't just react. Pause and make a decision.

REFLECTION

What stands out to me in this Reflection? What do I need to Change to Live this Fully? How will I Live this Today?

AUGUST 29

It's soooooo easy to see the wrong of others and say something. But make sure you acknowledge your wrong "first". It will "temper" HOW you plan to say whatever you say. It might even make you CHOOSE to say nothing.

REFLECTION

What stands out to me in this Reflection? What do I need to Change to Live this Fully? How will I Live this Today?

AUGUST 30

BE CAREFUL! Don't let "experiences" of betrayal, anger, hurt, infidelity, parent baggage, etc. make DECISIONS for you. Your TRUTH is your DECIDING factor. Experiences are just that experiences. Learn from them but don't be CONTROLLED by them.

REFLECTION

What stands out to me in this Reflection? What do I need to Change to Live this Fully? How will I Live this Today?

AUGUST 31

Sometimes we are trying so hard to get to where we are going that we forget to live. LIVING is apart of the journey.

REFLECTION

What stands out to me in this Reflection? What do I need to Change to Live this Fully? How will I Live this Today?

SEPTEMBER 1

A lot of people will NOT get "delivered" in a church service or at a altar. There are those who get set free eating dinner talking to someone, a business meeting, at the beauty salon, a theatre watching a play, a women's center in a workshop, a retreat, or on the PHONE! Ministry is not "limited" or only defined by a church "building" experience AND the church diaspora does not have a monopoly on the WORD ministry

REFLECTION

What stands out to me in this Reflection? What do I need to Change to Live this Fully? How will I Live this Today?

SEPTEMBER 2

Don't let your DISAPPOINTMENT in someone get you off focus. Don't CLOUD your mind with unanswerable questions regarding HOW they could make that decision. Don't be SHOCKED that they said that about you. Don't be PERPLEXED about them knowing better. If all of that is true, they were not ignorant when they made THAT decision.

REFLECTION

What stands out to me in this Reflection? What do I need to Change to Live this Fully? How will I Live this Today?

SEPTEMBER 3

You can't effectively MOVE forward and LOOK back at the same time. Do the work. Let IT Go. Refocus and Press FORWARD!

REFLECTION

What stands out to me in this Reflection? What do I need to Change to Live this Fully? How will I Live this Today?

SEPTEMBER 4

One of the hardest things you will ever do is look at yourself and be honest about what you see.

REFLECTION

What stands out to me in this Reflection? What do I need to Change to Live this Fully? How will I Live this Today?

SEPTEMBER 5

Stop saying you "don't do women"! All women are not immature, insecure and caddy. If you always end up in these type of relationships or you "never" seem to find empowering women..... the question becomes "what's going on within YOU that you "always" end up with rotten apples

REFLECTION

What stands out to me in this Reflection? What do I need to Change to Live this Fully? How will I Live this Today?

SEPTEMBER 6

Being "interested" doesn't help you "accomplish" what you need. Some people stay in "interested" mode and become comfortable and MISS opportunity. Then turn around and say, "I KNEW I should have done that". You can't stay there. You must learn the LESSON of making "committed" DECISIONs in order to move forward. Manifestation is the result of DECISIONS.

REFLECTION

What stands out to me in this Reflection? What do I need to Change to Live this Fully? How will I Live this Today?

SEPTEMBER 7

Pride will make you do and say "stupid" things to protect what should not be protected. Don't go down the rabbit trail.

REFLECTION

What stands out to me in this Reflection? What do I need to Change to Live this Fully? How will I Live this Today?

SEPTEMBER 8

When will you be important enough? When will you make time? The things and people that you are putting ahead of "you" developing yourself NEED YOU AS YOUR BEST SELF. Right now the only thing you can offer is "what could be". Rethink your perspective of putting "yourself" off. NOW is the time to BECOME your BEST, because they need you NOW not later.

REFLECTION

What stands out to me in this Reflection? What do I need to Change to Live this Fully? How will I Live this Today?

SEPTEMBER 9

When you don't know where you are headed, it is easy to get DISTRACTED by the different circumstances that come up in your life. The DISTRACTION can 1. begin looking like a "solution" or 2. keep you from FOCUSING on what is important. Be careful and remind yourself where you are going

REFLECTION

What stands out to me in this Reflection? What do I need to Change to Live this Fully? How will I Live this Today?

SEPTEMBER 10

Live AUTHENTIC so the people who are suppose to be in your life will COME, and those who won't accept you for you will GO. Don't let the circumstances of life "ENSLAVE" you because you are unwilling to invest to get the KNOWLEDGE necessary to be FREE. Don't SETTLE with making decisions with assumption and guessing as a "SOURCE of information". You don't have 2.

REFLECTION

What stands out to me in this Reflection? What do I need to Change to Live this Fully? How will I Live this Today?

SEPTEMBER 11

Do you have the "routine" of "waiting" for someone to go with you to get what YOU know you need? The lesson you NEED for your "next" might be for you to GO in spite of and THAT is why you can't find anyone to go with you. Step out!

REFLECTION

What stands out to me in this Reflection? What do I need to Change to Live this Fully? How will I Live this Today?

SEPTEMBER 12

Don't get in the habit of quitting and convincing yourself that "starting over" is the answer when it gets hard. A lot of times you have to push thru the hard part and keep going.

REFLECTION

What stands out to me in this Reflection? What do I need to Change to Live this Fully? How will I Live this Today?

SEPTEMBER 13

Our DREAMS do NOT have to REMAIN in our thoughts. We don't have to look and only dream about them in our minds like looking in a store window "wishing" we could have them. There is a WAY!!! The key is learning and moving on it. Do NOT accept the "window shopping experience" regarding your DREAMS (looking but not believing you can have it). DETERMINE TODAY that it will be more than just a picture in your mind. Say it with me, " I CAN have it!!"

REFLECTION

What stands out to me in this Reflection? What do I need to Change to Live this Fully? How will I Live this Today?

SEPTEMBER 14

Be mindful asking people in your last season to give you insight into a season God is taking you into and they have no knowledge, experience, insight or wisdom to instruct you about it. Don't let fear and the comfort of familiarity keep you from the "new" relationships you need for where you are going.

REFLECTION

What stands out to me in this Reflection? What do I need to Change to Live this Fully? How will I Live this Today?

SEPTEMBER 15

STOP waiting for other people to "value" you before you accept that you are valuable. It begins with YOU knowing your worth.

REFLECTION

What stands out to me in this Reflection? What do I need to Change to Live this Fully? How will I Live this Today?

SEPTEMBER 16

Say it with me, "What I am seeking is seeking after me." Yessss!!! Be in a place of expectation. Settle your heart that it is true AND coming. PREPARE and be ready for it. See it in your minds eye (imagination). It IS so!!

REFLECTION

What stands out to me in this Reflection? What do I need to Change to Live this Fully? How will I Live this Today?

SEPTEMBER 17

Change is necessary in order to see another outcome in your life. Its not just about your behavior. Change begins WITHIN with your beliefs and mindset ABOUT what you want to change

REFLECTION

What stands out to me in this Reflection? What do I need to Change to Live this Fully? How will I Live this Today?

SEPTEMBER 18

STOP waiting for someone else to DO what God has put in your heart, because you've never seen it done before! BE the FORERUNNER He has called you to be! You are a LEADER not a FOLLOWER.
STOP giving up your position

REFLECTION

What stands out to me in this Reflection? What do I need to Change to Live this Fully? How will I Live this Today?

SEPTEMBER 19

The "dry place" doesn't feel good BUT if you refuse to let it "bind" your mind because you don't have answers, you can become sensitive enough to hear the answers when they come.

REFLECTION

What stands out to me in this Reflection? What do I need to Change to Live this Fully? How will I Live this Today?

SEPTEMBER 20

There is "rain" for your dry place! Take out your umbrella. Expectation is powerful. Don't let "GOLIATH" (challenge/fear) tell you which direction to go! INTIMIDATION is his "greatest" weapon. If you are suppose to go thru the door he is standing in front of, TELL HIM TO MOVE and pick up your STONES!! Any other door will take you where you should NOT be. There is a way.

REFLECTION

What stands out to me in this Reflection? What do I need to Change to Live this Fully? How will I Live this Today?

SEPTEMBER 21

You are UNIQUE.
Don't "reduce" yourself by comparing yourself to someone else

REFLECTION

What stands out to me in this Reflection? What do I need to Change to Live this Fully? How will I Live this Today?

SEPTEMBER 22

When you give your word you are creating expectation. Because there is expectation you have a "responsibility" to VOLUNTEER information regarding that commitment. The person should not have to chase you or even ask YOU for a "update". It must become a understanding that it is YOUR responsibility to do so or "release" the person from the expectation.

REFLECTION

What stands out to me in this Reflection? What do I need to Change to Live this Fully? How will I Live this Today?

SEPTEMBER 23

It is easy to let our "appearance" become our "false" IDENTITY because we don't know who we really are. So we "borrow" from others what we desire or "dream" for ourselves. We use designer clothes (fake designer when we can't afford it lol), false nails, eye lashes, the "right" friends, beautiful robes, suits and fake personalities or personas. It is done, all in a "ATTEMPT" TO "CREATE" a Identity based on what we "wish" we could be. Don't settle for being fake or living as "false evidence." We can BECOME the AUTHENTIC and REAL thing but we must believe we can. Tooo many are settling because if the truth be told, they don't believe they can and are willing to settle with being fake

REFLECTION
What stands out to me in this Reflection? What do I need to Change to Live this Fully? How will I Live this Today?

SEPTEMBER 24

When working TOWARDS a goal, a ROUTINE is the answer to
"indecisiveness" (should I shouldn't I). You don't have to ask yourself if you are
going to do it, IT IS what you do

REFLECTION

What stands out to me in this Reflection? What do I need to Change to Live this Fully? How will I Live this Today?

SEPTEMBER 25

We ALL fantasize about what we want, but there comes a time when you ACT so you can see the manifestation of the DREAM . Don't allow the "fantasy" to become ENOUGH TO SATISFY your desire. Position yourself for its REALITY.

REFLECTION

What stands out to me in this Reflection? What do I need to Change to Live this Fully? How will I Live this Today?

SEPTEMBER 26

You MUST become a LIFE LONG LEARNER if you want more. Connect to the people and places that help you do it. Don't limit yourself.

REFLECTION

What stands out to me in this Reflection? What do I need to Change to Live this Fully? How will I Live this Today?

SEPTEMBER 27

When "everything " has to be done your way, you discover you end up DOING everything. Release the "control freak" and ALLOW others to take responsibility

REFLECTION

What stands out to me in this Reflection? What do I need to Change to Live this Fully? How will I Live this Today?

SEPTEMBER 28

A lot of times you "talk" to just be heard or to look the part. Sadly, in the depths of your heart you have no intentions of doing anything about what you are saying. The DANGEROUS part is that you have become a "hypocrite" TO YOURSELF, no one else. You've reduced the VALUE of your own words in YOUR EARS. The result, "needing" someone else to "speak" into your life because you have reduced the IMPACT of your own words regarding yourself TO yourself.

REFLECTION

What stands out to me in this Reflection? What do I need to Change to Live this Fully? How will I Live this Today?

SEPTEMBER 29

When YOU become truly important to you, and you understand that you CAN NOT fulfill your purpose without FIRST working on being WHOLE.... you will continue to "wait" for the right time, not realizing that NOW is ALWAYS the time to grow.

REFLECTION

What stands out to me in this Reflection? What do I need to Change to Live this Fully? How will I Live this Today?

SEPTEMBER 30

Going in the right direction doesn't mean you will not have challenges along the way! Don't let the presence of challenges convince you otherwise

REFLECTION

What stands out to me in this Reflection? What do I need to Change to Live this Fully? How will I Live this Today?

OCTOBER 1

There is no HONOR in self neglect. We were taught that it was "noble or what we do". We WILL change that narrative!! A self neglected, tired, frustrated, overweight, overworked, under appreciated woman will STOP being the STANDARD. It's SELFISH when you don't take care of yourself because what you COULD HAVE done is not accomplished

REFLECTION

What stands out to me in this Reflection? What do I need to Change to Live this Fully? How will I Live this Today?

OCTOBER 2

The "call and mandate" on your life won't look like everyone else's EVEN if you do the same type of "work". Don't let people put you in a BOX by trying to make you "look" like everyone else, because they don't get it. Don't DOUBT what your heart says is true. Do it the way God says DO IT. Don't QUESTION the difference between you and someone else... FLOW with it

REFLECTION

What stands out to me in this Reflection? What do I need to Change to Live this Fully? How will I Live this Today?

OCTOBER 3

"Make" yourself do what you are suppose to do regarding your goals. It is a decision. Yes, it is that simple. Decide TO DO it, instead of NOT TO DO it. You CHOOSE either way.

REFLECTION

What stands out to me in this Reflection? What do I need to Change to Live this Fully? How will I Live this Today?

OCTOBER 4

Don't be disheartened when the people who should see your greatness don't....
until strangers do. Know for YOURSELF who you are and it won't matter who
notices. Just make sure your pleasing your GREATEST audience.....GOD.

REFLECTION

What stands out to me in this Reflection? What do I need to Change to Live this Fully? How will I Live this Today?

OCTOBER 5

Your choices have RESULTS. Stop making FAITH about God "getting rid" of the consequences of your actions. Learn to make CHOICES that manifest the results you desire. Elevate FAITH to being a "support" to your choices and about God HONORING His word in your life, NOT RESCUING you because you want to do what you want WITHOUT consequences.

REFLECTION

What stands out to me in this Reflection? What do I need to Change to Live this Fully? How will I Live this Today?

OCTOBER 6

Your "mindset" will influence your decisions. Be aware! Are you looking at your circumstance thru the eyes (mindset) of lack, loss, poverty, victimization or wealth, victory, opportunity, success? It makes a HUGE difference!

REFLECTION

What stands out to me in this Reflection? What do I need to Change to Live this Fully? How will I Live this Today?

OCTOBER 7

There will ALWAYS be people who won't agree with you. Don't let that stop you from standing FIRM. But ALSO learn the "appropriate" time to defend. It's not always necessary.

REFLECTION

What stands out to me in this Reflection? What do I need to Change to Live this Fully? How will I Live this Today?

OCTOBER 8

SPEAK over your life (so your ears can hear). Don't just think over it
You need to hear YOUR declaration! SPEAK IT!

REFLECTION

What stands out to me in this Reflection? What do I need to Change to Live this Fully? How will I Live this Today?

OCTOBER 9

As you move into your "next level/season" remember, the habits/issues that you failed to address will begin to interfere. Why? because you need that discipline for the success of your next level/season! You should have dealt with it when you saw it. Discipline is your FRIEND not your enemy.

REFLECTION

What stands out to me in this Reflection? What do I need to Change to Live this Fully? How will I Live this Today?

OCTOBER 10

Make up your mind what's important. Don't become a member of "last minute ministry" and miss out on what you really want because you won't choose. Don't leave life up to CHANCE

REFLECTION
What stands out to me in this Reflection? What do I need to Change to Live this Fully? How will I Live this Today?

OCTOBER 11

Being a mom and "being" yourself doesn't have to be two separate things. To often we think we have to LOOSE ourselves in order to "be" a mom. We fail to realize that BEING ourselves empowers BEING a mom and our children. Being a mom is a ROLE you walk in, it is NOT who you are

REFLECTION

What stands out to me in this Reflection? What do I need to Change to Live this Fully? How will I Live this Today?

OCTOBER 12

Faith/Religion/Belief is not a "coping mechanism." It's not "one of many ways" to "fix" your problems or get "relief" FROM life. It is so much more. It is a way of being, thinking and living. It's connection to what is bigger than you. If it is only a way to "cope" you are missing the beautiful POWER of faith.

REFLECTION

What stands out to me in this Reflection? What do I need to Change to Live this Fully? How will I Live this Today?

OCTOBER 13

There will be people who will speak badly of you. There will be people who won't believe in your vision. Please deal with that because people don't have to like you. I know I know... you are nice and wonderful lol. Listen, You are not here to try to "impress" them, so DON'T live your life or make decisions trying to PROVE THEM WRONG. Be "settled" in who you are. Be "settled" in what God has spoken over your life. Be "settled" in your ability. Connect to those that SUPPORT and BELIEVE in you. Don't "depend" on negativity to motivate and "empower" your journey. Allow TRUTH to OPEN your sail.

REFLECTION

What stands out to me in this Reflection? What do I need to Change to Live this Fully? How will I Live this Today?

OCTOBER 14

Be mindful "waiting" to be appreciated in order to
"validate" your worth/value. YOU must be settled in
yourself about what you "bring to the table"

REFLECTION

What stands out to me in this Reflection? What do I need to Change to Live this Fully? How will I Live this Today?

OCTOBER 15

Don't allow people's emotional drama to BIND you. You will look up and find yourself in drama mode and wondering what's wrong with you!

REFLECTION

What stands out to me in this Reflection? What do I need to Change to Live this Fully? How will I Live this Today?

OCTOBER 16

Be mindful of "life" leaches. People who just "take". A lot of times they "look and act" like they NEED your help but KNOW that they never have the intention of having a relationship that causes them to give. They will suck out your life and resources. Then when you have nothing else to give them, they move on to the next person.

REFLECTION

What stands out to me in this Reflection? What do I need to Change to Live this Fully? How will I Live this Today?

OCTOBER 17

STOP giving yourself a "easy out". If it's not working change your plan. There is a answer, but YOU have to believe there is one. Quitting doesn't make it easier. It makes it take longer

REFLECTION

What stands out to me in this Reflection? What do I need to Change to Live this Fully? How will I Live this Today?

OCTOBER 18

Don't allow people to pull you into "emotional" drama (caused by their choices)
because they don't want to take responsibility. Hold onto your peace

REFLECTION

What stands out to me in this Reflection? What do I need to Change to Live this Fully? How will I Live this Today?

OCTOBER 19

You are not punishing the person that hurt you by "living miserable, angry, or broke down" (trying to show/remind them of the harm they did to you and your life). Living FREE and successful doesn't "let them off the hook"..... it RELEASES YOU! Be FREE!

REFLECTION

What stands out to me in this Reflection? What do I need to Change to Live this Fully? How will I Live this Today?

OCTOBER 20

Our ACTIONS are a testimony of what we BELIEVE is acceptable behavior
EVEN if we SAY something else. What do you "really" believe?

REFLECTION

What stands out to me in this Reflection? What do I need to Change to Live this Fully? How will I Live this Today?

OCTOBER 21

If you can't be corrected, how do you know if you are doing something wrong that really "needs" to change? Quality Correction should not be viewed as an attack and "offense" should not be the response. It should be a opportunity to learn and grow. If someone can't tell you the truth, you are in trouble. Breathe and listen.

REFLECTION

What stands out to me in this Reflection? What do I need to Change to Live this Fully? How will I Live this Today?

OCTOBER 22

Don't "determine" your change based on if someone else changes. This is about you.

REFLECTION

What stands out to me in this Reflection? What do I need to Change to Live this Fully? How will I Live this Today?

OCTOBER 23

When truth is not honored through action in our lives, it loses its authority and impact. Are you "living" your truth or is it just words that sound good to you? It must go beyond words.

REFLECTION

What stands out to me in this Reflection? What do I need to Change to Live this Fully? How will I Live this Today?

OCTOBER 24

Ask questions instead of assuming

REFLECTION

What stands out to me in this Reflection? What do I need to Change to Live this Fully? How will I Live this Today?

OCTOBER 25

Until you stop DENYING that YOU are important to your purpose,
you won't find it.

REFLECTION

What stands out to me in this Reflection? What do I need to Change to Live this Fully? How will I Live this Today?

OCTOBER 26

Step by step is how you do it. YESSS... the "big picture" looks sooo wonderful, but you got to take the FIRST step FIRST. NO, it is not as pretty as the end result but it is necessary. Don't skip the process thinking the "end" is the prize. It's the "steps" that have the VALUE.

REFLECTION

What stands out to me in this Reflection? What do I need to Change to Live this Fully? How will I Live this Today?

OCTOBER 27

Your "reactions" are YOURS. It is what you have given yourself PERMISSION to do. Be mindful blaming someone else for your choice. If it's not how you want to "act", intentionally choose another "reaction". Otherwise you have GIVEN someone else power they don't deserve.

REFLECTION

What stands out to me in this Reflection? What do I need to Change to Live this Fully? How will I Live this Today?

OCTOBER 28

Be mindful what you "meditate" on. You are a product of what you think. Make sure your thoughts are a reflection of who you want to be. Anything that does not support how you see yourself, refuse to allow it in your thought life

REFLECTION

What stands out to me in this Reflection? What do I need to Change to Live this Fully? How will I Live this Today?

OCTOBER 29

Learn to develop relationships that empower the DIFFERENT aspects of your life. Everyone doesn't have to be attached to everything you do.

REFLECTION

What stands out to me in this Reflection? What do I need to Change to Live this Fully? How will I Live this Today?

OCTOBER 30

Your RELATIONSHIPS are a REFLECTION and SUPPORT of your "insecurities" or your "strengths". Whichever is the STRONGEST will impact and DIRECT you (whether you realize it or not). Look at your company and ask the question, " Do you uphold/feed my insecurities or my strengths?"

REFLECTION

What stands out to me in this Reflection? What do I need to Change to Live this Fully? How will I Live this Today?

OCTOBER 31

It is very tempting to fall back into the habits of the past.
When tempted remind yourself why you decided to do something different

REFLECTION

What stands out to me in this Reflection? What do I need to Change to Live this Fully? How will I Live this Today?

NOVEMBER 1

You must reNEW your mind TOWARDS your NEW.
You can't keep the "old" mindset" and "expect" NEW things.

REFLECTION

What stands out to me in this Reflection? What do I need to Change to Live this Fully? How will I Live this Today?

NOVEMBER 2

Learn to enjoy your own company.

REFLECTION

What stands out to me in this Reflection? What do I need to Change to Live this Fully? How will I Live this Today?

NOVEMBER 3

Your "calling/message/Purpose" will make room for you.
No need to fight or beg. Just make sure you are Prepared!

REFLECTION

What stands out to me in this Reflection? What do I need to Change to Live this Fully? How will I Live this Today?

NOVEMBER 4

It's exciting and fun to TALK about your "new season", but it takes work to obtain and keep it. You can't stay the same.

REFLECTION

What stands out to me in this Reflection? What do I need to Change to Live this Fully? How will I Live this Today?

NOVEMBER 5

BEGIN where you are. STOP talking yourself out of your VISION because you want to "start" a different way (location, money, relationships). Where you are IS where you are and it doesn't have to stop you! Don't let that be an EXCUSE NOT to do what you can. There is SOMETHING in your NOW that will get you moving forward.

REFLECTION

What stands out to me in this Reflection? What do I need to Change to Live this Fully? How will I Live this Today?

NOVEMBER 6

There is MORE to it then just wanting it or wanting to do it. You have to be just as PASSIONATE about doing what is NECESSARY to get it.

REFLECTION

What stands out to me in this Reflection? What do I need to Change to Live this Fully? How will I Live this Today?

NOVEMBER 7

We GROW when we can hear the TRUTH about ourselves. Yes, the good but also the bad and the ugly! The key is not just to "hear" it but also to make a decision to do something about it.

REFLECTION

What stands out to me in this Reflection? What do I need to Change to Live this Fully? How will I Live this Today?

NOVEMBER 8

Learn to listen to your body if it says you need rest. It has no reason to lie to you

REFLECTION

What stands out to me in this Reflection? What do I need to Change to Live this Fully? How will I Live this Today?

NOVEMBER 9

EVERYTHING about you is "strategically designed" for your Purpose. When you DISCOVER and begin to KNOW your UNIQUE IDENTITY and how to "release" it into the world, your IMPACT will be UNDENIABLE.

REFLECTION

What stands out to me in this Reflection? What do I need to Change to Live this Fully? How will I Live this Today?

NOVEMBER 10

It is very possible for a FRIEND not to be your PURPOSE partner. You might need to separate those relationships. Everyone can't handle your Vision.
Yes, even a friend.

REFLECTION

What stands out to me in this Reflection? What do I need to Change to Live this Fully? How will I Live this Today?

NOVEMBER 11

Get to the point that you "embrace" and "enjoy" moving away from the things that don't honor your journey. It is NOT a loss.... you GAIN.

REFLECTION

What stands out to me in this Reflection? What do I need to Change to Live this Fully? How will I Live this Today?

NOVEMBER 12

You have ONE life. When are you going to POSITION yourself and begin to LIVE and not just exist? Sometimes we act like we have a long time but we don't. The time is NOW!! Don't leave the earth with your PURPOSE unexpressed.

REFLECTION

What stands out to me in this Reflection? What do I need to Change to Live this Fully? How will I Live this Today?

NOVEMBER 13

There is GRACE for your circumstance. Allow your confidence in TRUTH to "release" expectation, that it WILL come together for your good

REFLECTION

What stands out to me in this Reflection? What do I need to Change to Live this Fully? How will I Live this Today?

NOVEMBER 14

When you WRITE OUT your thoughts and the issues of the situation you are facing, it makes it easier to process what you are dealing with. Why? because you can't change the "facts". As long as it is in your head, you can "manipulate" it to "fit" whatever scenario is running thru your mind. Learn to journal.

REFLECTION

What stands out to me in this Reflection? What do I need to Change to Live this Fully? How will I Live this Today?

NOVEMBER 15

Stop trying to SALVAGE things (relationships, circumstances) in your life that need to DIE. It is HOLDING UP future possibilities. It is like a flower dying in the garden. You need to PRUNE it so the new flower can have SPACE to grow.

REFLECTION

What stands out to me in this Reflection? What do I need to Change to Live this Fully? How will I Live this Today?

NOVEMBER 16

If you don't know your PURPOSE and MESSAGE... You need to ASK for help!
Time is moving. Don't DEPRIVE me and others of the ideas, books, wisdom,
inventions and empowerment you were   CALLED to impart!

REFLECTION

What stands out to me in this Reflection? What do I need to Change to Live this Fully? How will I Live this Today?

NOVEMBER 17

We must learn to stop OVERTHINKING things. Be mindful making the SIMPLE...COMPLICATED. Sometimes we do this because we fear or we are insecure about making a decision.

REFLECTION

What stands out to me in this Reflection? What do I need to Change to Live this Fully? How will I Live this Today?

NOVEMBER 18

The "healing process" doesn't have to be a time of being "stuck or immobile".
You can grow as you heal.

REFLECTION

What stands out to me in this Reflection? What do I need to Change to Live this Fully? How will I Live this Today?

NOVEMBER 19

You know the VERY sad part about Women who are so insecure they feel the need to compete, bad mouth or copy you is? THEY CAN HAVE THEIR OWN!! There is a BEAUTIFUL, ABUNDANT, POWERFUL vision with their name on it and NO ONE will be able to compare. But their focus is on someone's else's stuff and they miss out on ALL they could be

REFLECTION

What stands out to me in this Reflection? What do I need to Change to Live this Fully? How will I Live this Today?

NOVEMBER 20

Whatever you did to GET there you will have to do to STAY. If you plan on a permanent change and not just a temporary "fix" you must plan wisely and make sure you are willing to keep it up!

REFLECTION

What stands out to me in this Reflection? What do I need to Change to Live this Fully? How will I Live this Today?

Being MEEK doesn't mean WEAK or that you let people "run over you". Being MEEK means you are patient and IN CONTROL of yourself EVEN when being PROVOKED. You know what to say and when to say it. You know how to be HUMBLE in ANY circumstance, because you know who you are and are not DEFINED by others opinion. You know that your REACTION says something about you. You choose to REACT in a way that brings LIFE to the situation.

REFLECTION

What stands out to me in this Reflection? What do I need to Change to Live this Fully? How will I Live this Today?

NOVEMBER 22

Take "authority" over the stories of your past, that "just come up" to be a distraction when you are trying to PRESS forward to your future. Don't shut down.

REFLECTION

What stands out to me in this Reflection? What do I need to Change to Live this Fully? How will I Live this Today?

NOVEMBER 23

Can you trust yourself to keep your word TO yourself? It's interesting how much we lie to OURSELVES, then expect that "same mouth" to have spiritual authority FOR ourself. Your word matters.

REFLECTION

What stands out to me in this Reflection? What do I need to Change to Live this Fully? How will I Live this Today?

NOVEMBER 24

I have learned that PURPOSE begins with developing WHO we are not just WHAT we do. It is through developing WHO we are that we begin to fulfill our destiny and purpose and that is what makes what we do meaningful and effective

REFLECTION

What stands out to me in this Reflection? What do I need to Change to Live this Fully? How will I Live this Today?

NOVEMBER 25

Part of becoming your BEST SELF is DEALING WITH your baggage. Stop hiding behind scriptures, pretending you are changing. The Bible is a ACTION PLAN. Do the work.

REFLECTION

What stands out to me in this Reflection? What do I need to Change to Live this Fully? How will I Live this Today?

NOVEMBER 26

Organization is necessary for sustained growth. It's time to get organized.

REFLECTION

What stands out to me in this Reflection? What do I need to Change to Live this Fully? How will I Live this Today?

NOVEMBER 27

YOU have a part to play in your SUCCESS. Yes, God opens doors, but I PROMISE you, He will NOT open doors you are not ready for (if He did you couldn't stay if you weren't ready). So the question then becomes, are you opening the doors because you want to GO, or are the doors OPENING because you are ready. THAT PART is on you.

REFLECTION

What stands out to me in this Reflection? What do I need to Change to Live this Fully? How will I Live this Today?

NOVEMBER 28

Don't wait for people to believe in your VISION. Runnnnnnnn! Their approval doesn't make it legitimate! No one will ever want your visions success more than you!! Believe in yourself and Runnnnnnn!!!!!

REFLECTION

What stands out to me in this Reflection? What do I need to Change to Live this Fully? How will I Live this Today?

NOVEMBER 29

Be careful of the voices (people or mindset) that try to come into your PRESENT and pull you BACK to a time when THEY had influence in your life by "downgrading" the importance of your NOW.

REFLECTION

What stands out to me in this Reflection? What do I need to Change to Live this Fully? How will I Live this Today?

NOVEMBER 30

DISTRACTIONS aren't always things that are BAD. It might "really" be something you need to do. BUT, they are distractions because they keep you from where you intended to go. They break your focus and "tempt" you to make another decision IN SPITE of what you already decided to do. IT IS STILL a distraction.

REFLECTION

What stands out to me in this Reflection? What do I need to Change to Live this Fully? How will I Live this Today?

DECEMBER 1

When you don't "self care" (Spirit Soul and Body) YOU are saying that you are inconvenient.... everything/person carries more "value" than you. How? You've GIVEN it/them priority.

REFLECTION

What stands out to me in this Reflection? What do I need to Change to Live this Fully? How will I Live this Today?

DECEMBER 2

Self Care is not just about getting your hair and nails done (it can include that).
Self Care is taking the NECESSARY time and action to do what you need to make
sure you can function at your best.

REFLECTION

What stands out to me in this Reflection? What do I need to Change to Live this Fully? How will I Live this Today?

DECEMBER 3

Guard your heart in every conversation.

REFLECTION

What stands out to me in this Reflection? What do I need to Change to Live this Fully? How will I Live this Today?

DECEMBER 4

In order to enjoy your life, you must give yourself permission to be YOURSELF.
For in "being" YOU the mask are removed and there is FREEDOM.

REFLECTION

What stands out to me in this Reflection? What do I need to Change to Live this Fully? How will I Live this Today?

DECEMBER 5

DON'T QUIT! Press beyond your emotions. Get FOCUSED on where you want to BE. Ignore the DISTRACTIONS. Make up your MIND to succeed

REFLECTION

What stands out to me in this Reflection? What do I need to Change to Live this Fully? How will I Live this Today?

DECEMBER 6

When you are not PREPARED, you make a MESS. It might not show up in the "short" term but BELIEVE me, it will show up. PREPARE for the VISION that is before you. Don't "neglect" the necessary. It's tedious because it's vital to the LONG term success of your vision.

REFLECTION

What stands out to me in this Reflection? What do I need to Change to Live this Fully? How will I Live this Today?

DECEMBER 7

Celebrate your victories no matter how small they are. They add up! Then when the sad times come you can "remember" and encourage yourself to keep moving.

REFLECTION

What stands out to me in this Reflection? What do I need to Change to Live this Fully? How will I Live this Today?

DECEMBER 8

You can't do more for people than what they are willing to do for themselves. When the excuses start flowing from them...... pause. They have to want it. It's hard at first but you have to release people to their choice. It must be their choice because it's their life. You support.
You don't take on someone else's responsibility for their lives.

REFLECTION

What stands out to me in this Reflection? What do I need to Change to Live this Fully? How will I Live this Today?

DECEMBER 9

We need people to "do life with." Paul said I'm not in your life just to teach you the Bible, I want to "do life with you". I just LOVE that. Who are you doing life with? Not church attendance..LIFE. Healthy Faith-filled Empowering Relationships are so important. People that speak to you Spirit Soul and Body. People that speak to your DESTINY and FORWARD movement.
These people are necessary.

REFLECTION

What stands out to me in this Reflection? What do I need to Change to Live this Fully? How will I Live this Today?

DECEMBER 10

Making people feel "ignorant" doesn't LEGITIMIZE your position.
Teach don't BEAT. HONEY taste better.

REFLECTION

What stands out to me in this Reflection? What do I need to Change to Live this Fully? How will I Live this Today?

DECEMBER 11

Don't pretend anymore. The real definition of excuse is "I don't want to do it ENOUGH to do it."
Stop trying to make the excuse sound meaningful.

REFLECTION

What stands out to me in this Reflection? What do I need to Change to Live this Fully? How will I Live this Today?

DECEMBER 12

Don't be ashamed to begin again. It's better to admit you are going in the wrong direction, then to keep going because you are concerned about what people think.

REFLECTION

What stands out to me in this Reflection? What do I need to Change to Live this Fully? How will I Live this Today?

DECEMBER 13

Everyone won't understand your VISION. Stop feeling obligated to explain yourself to people who REALLY don't want to know. They prefer to believe the lie because it justifies their baggage or opinion. STAND knowing that your steps are ordered by God for the people HE has called you to reach

REFLECTION

What stands out to me in this Reflection? What do I need to Change to Live this Fully? How will I Live this Today?

DECEMBER 14

Create HARMONY in your life by understanding that everything doesn't carry the same "priority value" at the same time. When you try to "balance" you are saying that EVERYTHING carries the same "priority value", So you end up trying to do EVERYTHING. It doesn't work like that. Analyze what has "priority value" based on the season you are in and you won't be overwhelmed. It ebbs and flows. Make sure YOUR personal time is ALWAYS A PART of it.

REFLECTION

What stands out to me in this Reflection? What do I need to Change to Live this Fully? How will I Live this Today?

DECEMBER 15

Don't put yourself "down" in order to "appreciate" someone at your expense.
You can appreciate them and KEEP your value!

REFLECTION

What stands out to me in this Reflection? What do I need to Change to Live this Fully? How will I Live this Today?

DECEMBER 16

The true fight is standing in CONFIDENCE and TRUST in what God said not what the enemy is doing. We must become more God conscious than enemy conscious. FOCUS on standing on what God SAID about your circumstance and not the DISTRACTIONS that are trying to keep you from it!

REFLECTION

What stands out to me in this Reflection? What do I need to Change to Live this Fully? How will I Live this Today?

DECEMBER 17

Why do we choose to NOT be a PRIORITY in our OWN lives? Without "self care" Spirit Soul and Body you are of "less" impact in others. Why? Because you are not your optimal self and therefore those in your life are impacted.

REFLECTION

What stands out to me in this Reflection? What do I need to Change to Live this Fully? How will I Live this Today?

DECEMBER 18

Don't make decisions when your emotions are high.
Make decisions from your TRUTH.

REFLECTION

What stands out to me in this Reflection? What do I need to Change to Live this Fully? How will I Live this Today?

DECEMBER 19

Your word matters, not just towards others but in your OWN ears.

REFLECTION

What stands out to me in this Reflection? What do I need to Change to Live this Fully? How will I Live this Today?

DECEMBER 20

SUCCESS begins with believing that it is possible! I am not talking about hoping or wishing. I am talking about YOU believing. YOU accepting that it is TRUE and not wavering. YOU not being moved by what you see, and NOT what someone told you "about" yourself. lol. YOU have to believe it can be.

REFLECTION

What stands out to me in this Reflection? What do I need to Change to Live this Fully? How will I Live this Today?

DECEMBER 21

Don't LOOSE yourself trying to be EVERYTHING for everyone else. If you are not careful you will look up and find yourself wondering who you really are.

REFLECTION

What stands out to me in this Reflection? What do I need to Change to Live this Fully? How will I Live this Today?

DECEMBER 22

Some of your "friends/family" don't have the ABILITY to support your dream/vision. It is not about love it is about capacity and perspective. Just because they love you doesn't mean they know "how" to support where you are going. Find the people "called" to your dream/vision.

REFLECTION

What stands out to me in this Reflection? What do I need to Change to Live this Fully? How will I Live this Today?

DECEMBER 23

Learning to honor your TRUTH "in spite" of others and being able to tell the difference between someone's opinion and wisdom is important for your journey.

REFLECTION

What stands out to me in this Reflection? What do I need to Change to Live this Fully? How will I Live this Today?

DECEMBER 24

Some people are not "healthy" enough (emotionally, mentally, personally) to be in a relationship with you. They can't "handle" seeing you move forward or grow. STOP forcing these relationships. Is there potential? Yes. Is it suppose to be? Maybe. That is not the REAL question. The REAL question is can THEY handle it.

REFLECTION

What stands out to me in this Reflection? What do I need to Change to Live this Fully? How will I Live this Today?

DECEMBER 25

Learn to make up your own mind. Getting advice is good, but it should compliment what you want. Living your life waiting on someone to tell you what to do is a sign of insecurity...or FEAR. You shouldn't just ABRUPTLY change direction bc someone doesn't agree. You need to have some idea what you want.

REFLECTION

What stands out to me in this Reflection? What do I need to Change to Live this Fully? How will I Live this Today?

DECEMBER 26

It's important to be around people whose very presence/influence "challenges"
your "status quo/comfort zone" WITHOUT even saying a word.
It is their VERY presence/influence that "stirs" you to do and BE better.

REFLECTION

What stands out to me in this Reflection? What do I need to Change to Live this Fully? How will I Live this Today?

DECEMBER 27

It is sooo sad to see women who "desire" to change their lives BUT won't do anything about it. They "passively" wait to be rescued and unconsciously believe that it is someone else's responsibility to do it. The real sad part is... no one can rescue you, you MUST rescue and take the INITIATIVE to change yourself.

REFLECTION

What stands out to me in this Reflection? What do I need to Change to Live this Fully? How will I Live this Today?

DECEMBER 28

STOP chasing people who have NO INTENTIONS of being caught or who PLAY GAMES with your EMOTIONS because of their INSECURITY. Take them at their WORD even if you THINK or KNOW they don't mean it. YOU teach people how to treat you by your REACTION to their ACTIONS

REFLECTION
What stands out to me in this Reflection? What do I need to Change to Live this Fully? How will I Live this Today?

DECEMBER 29

Your PERSPECTIVE of your circumstance will DETERMINE the decisions you make about your circumstance. STOP focusing on why it won't work and begin FOCUSING and BELIEVING why it will! As I always say, "What you focus on GROWS!" Allow the GOOD to grow.

REFLECTION

What stands out to me in this Reflection? What do I need to Change to Live this Fully? How will I Live this Today?

DECEMBER 30

When you are moving to your GREATER there is always a activity you need to do that you don't like. Don't avoid it! It's NECESSARY for the process. Change your thinking about it. Begin seeing and purposefully desire the benefits.

REFLECTION

What stands out to me in this Reflection? What do I need to Change to Live this Fully? How will I Live this Today?

DECEMBER 31

Remind yourself EVERYDAY "where" you are headed and "why" you are doing it!

REFLECTION

What stands out to me in this Reflection? What do I need to Change to Live this Fully? How will I Live this Today?

Made in the USA
Middletown, DE
24 October 2023

41300906R00210